IMAGES of America
BIG SPRING AND HOWARD COUNTY

IMAGES of America
BIG SPRING AND HOWARD COUNTY

Tammy Burrow Schrecengost

Copyright © 2002 by Tammy Burrow Schrecengost
ISBN 978-0-7385-2059-9

Published by Arcadia Publishing
Charleston, South Carolina

Printed in the United States of America

Library of Congress Catalog Card Number: 2002103217

For all general information contact Arcadia Publishing at:
Telephone 843-853-2070
Fax 843-853-0044
E-mail sales@arcadiapublishing.com
For customer service and orders:
Toll-Free 1-888-313-2665

Visit us on the Internet at www.arcadiapublishing.com

Contents

Acknowledgments 6

Introduction 7

1. Downtown Big Spring 9
2. Local Folks 35
3. Homes on the Range 47
4. Life on the Ranch 65
5. Railroad 73
6. It's a Gusher 83
7. We Praise, Learn, and Teach 91
8. Hotel, Motel, and Tourist Courts 103
9. Let the Good Times Roll 117
10. World War I to Webb A.F.B. 123

Acknowledgments

Jerry Worthy and a small group of newly organized board members founded the Heritage Museum in 1971. Big Spring and Howard County residents have given their time and donations to continually improve this wonderful establishment. I am privileged and honored to work in such a historically significant environment. I love the history and life stories of each individual that make up this small community, and have undying gratitude to the people who took the photographs that recorded those unforgettable moments in time. A special thanks go to the Bradshaw sisters who recorded 53 years of Big Spring and Howard County life. With a click of a button they captured pool openings, beauty queens, burning buildings, sandstorms, floods, politicians, trains, and notable people throughout the world, as well as the community. Through the careful preservation of the museum, their contributions will be shared for many years to come.

I wish I could have used all of the photographs that depict the early years in Howard County. I give special thanks to Joe Pickle, the late Shine Philips and Polly Mays, Nila Allen, Charlene Ragen, Tito Arencibia, and the Howard County Historical Society, for recording past events and telling the stories of days gone by. My deepest gratitude goes to Nancy Raney for all of her help during the compilation of this book, curator Beth Purcell, who encouraged me to do this book, and to former curator, Angela Way, who gave me invaluable experience and guidance.

I owe special gratitude to Keith Ulrich and Arcadia Publishing for helping me and for publishing a book that will be around for Howard County's future generations.

I dedicate this book to my three children Ethan, Kristen, and Magen; my granddaughter Mckenzie; my father, Richard Burrow; my brother and sister-in-law, Mike and Shelley Burrow; my grandmother, Juanice Carter; and to all the people of Big Spring and Howard County who labored through hardships and celebrated in triumph to make this community what it is today.

Finally, I dedicate this book in memory of my mother Betty Sue Burrow and my brother Richard Gregg Burrow, who shared with me the love of history and the unquenchable desire to learn more about the past.

Tammy Burrow Schrecengost
March 2002

INTRODUCTION

Captain Randolph Barnes Marcy was the first man to discover the "big spring" on October 3, 1849. In a detailed diary, Marcy describes his parties' arrival at the spring. He said they had traveled over a beautiful road that brought them to a spring flowing over a deep chasm in the limestone rocks. Although Marcy first discovered the springs, the Native Americans had long known of the oasis. The "big spring" was at the crossroads of the Comanche War Trail. The Kiowas, Apaches, and Comanches all camped at the spring; however the Comanches had unquestionable reign over the "big spring" country. The Quahadis, a band of Comanches led by Quanah Parker, were the last to surrender to the reservations in 1875. By this time, hunters had already destroyed the buffalo, the Indian's main source of food, clothing, and shelter. From 1871–74, approximately 4.5 million buffalo were slaughtered, forcing the starving Indians onto government reservations. The buffalo bones were scattered across the plains in vast quantities when settlers began collecting and selling them.

The first settlers in Howard County were David Abner Rhoton and W.T. (Bud) Roberts. They both moved their families on land located at Moss Springs in the early 1880s and began ranching.

A "tent city" was built at the springs while waiting for the railroad to arrive. In 1881, Jay Gould, president of T&P Railroad, had a work crew pushing into Big Spring. The tent city pulled up their stakes and moved two miles north to the site of the future railroad in Sulphur Draw (Beals Creek). Once the railroad finally arrived and began service, Big Spring started to erect more permanent dwellings. Schools were established to educate the young, and a newspaper, *The Pantagraph*, was started by a lawyer and a preacher. Churches were organized by different faiths, hotels were built, and banks were formed. Law and government were established and a courthouse and jail were constructed, and homesteaders began claiming land for farming and ranching.

Big Spring enjoyed the profits of "Black Gold" when oil was discovered in 1925. The Great Depression was not felt as harshly in Big Spring as in other areas, but building expansion halted by 1930. After World War II erupted, trains were in full use, hauling troops and materials. Cosden Petroleum Corporation had maximized its production, and the U.S. Army selected Big Spring to be home of the bombardier school. In 1952, Webb A.F.B. opened and trained pilots from around the world until its closure in 1977.

On October 3, 1949, Big Spring celebrated the Centennial with a production of the Centurama, a re-enactment of the discovery of Big Spring by Marcy, and a week of celebrations. In 1981, a Centennial commemorated the arrival of the railroad and the beginning of Big Spring and Howard County. The Big Spring Cowboy Reunion and Rodeo was organized in 1933, and is still performed every June. Locals formed clubs and organizations to aid in the growth and well-being of the community. In 1945, voters approved the creation of the Howard

County Junior College District, and in 1980, Southwest Collegiate Institute for the Deaf. SWCID opened a school for the hearing impaired.

Big Spring became the headquarters for the Colorado River Municipal Water District, which supplies water to eight cities as well as seventeen oil and industrial companies. In 1978, facilities at the recently closed Webb AFB were used to house the Federal Correctional Prison and five Cornell Correctional Centers were later added.

Three towns, Big Spring, Coahoma, and Forsan, and seven communities, Lomax, Elbow, Garden City, Knott, Vealmoor, Ackerly, and Vincent, make up Howard County. These small communities and towns pulled together to improve and grow. The 1881 pioneer paved the way for our advancement and growth. May we always continue to build our community with faith, perseverance, optimism, and endurance.

One
DOWNTOWN BIG SPRING

In the early 1880s, settlers made their way west to Big Spring. Most went to work for the T&P Railroad, which provided a nice stable income. Others established ranches on the rich grazing land. Later, businesses, schools, and local government sprang up, and Big Spring was on its way to becoming a viable community.

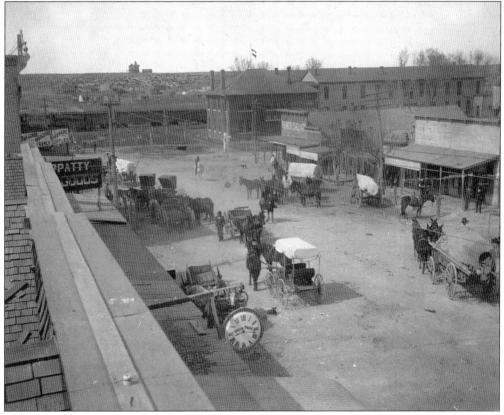

1902 MAIN STREET. By 1902, this dusty Big Spring Main Street was lined with simple wooden structures with false-front facades. (Reid Collection, Heritage Museum.)

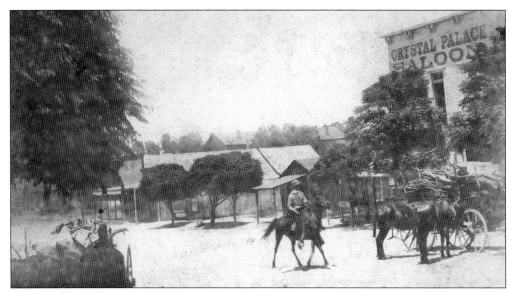

CRYSTAL PALACE SALOON. In 1894, The Crystal Palace Saloon was one of 13 saloons located in Big Spring. The bartenders often tried to persuade the mischievous cowboy to check his gun in at the bar, but few did. Instead, several of those cowpokes would shoot out the back mirrors and the lights, after too many 10¢ beers. Most cowboys were remorseful and agreed to pick up the tab. Some of the more "classier" saloons kept spare mirrors in the back, knowing that temptation would rule out. (Heritage Museum.)

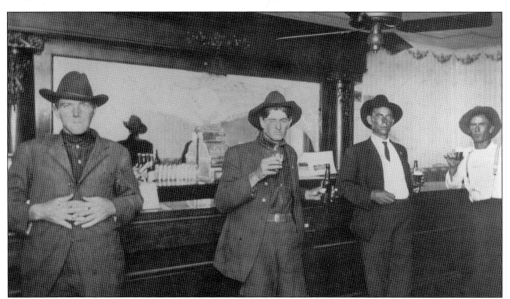

COWBOYS AT BAR. The saloon had a bar stretching across one side of the room with a brass rail at the bottom, for cowpunchers to hook their heels over, and later in the evening the bar enabled them to stand. These cowboys, including Sterling Price (far right), had shaken off the dust from the McDowell ranch, and put their city clothes on for a night on the town. Ed Wheat's Ranch Saloon was a favorite stop for the cowboys until Ed met his untimely death, in Big Spring's first "shoot out" with Sheriff J.A. Baggett on November 26, 1903. (Tucker Collection, Heritage Museum.)

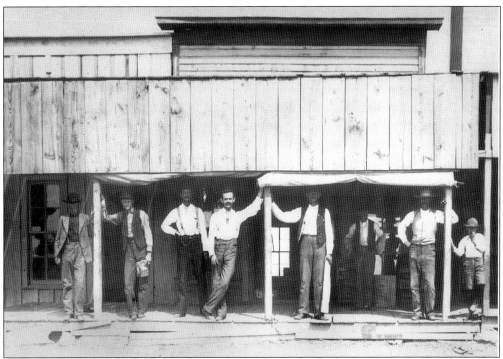

COWBOYS AT THE RANCH SALOON. Cowboys and saloonkeepers gather in front of the Ranch Saloon for a photograph. It was said "most of the cowboys were always gentlemen and the bad ones didn't last long around here." On occasion, a cowboy might get a little too frisky and ride into the saloon on his horse, but no harm was done. (Heritage Museum.)

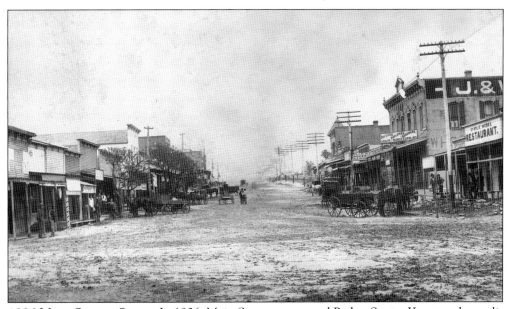

1906 MAIN STREET SCENE. In 1906, Main Street was named Parker Street. Kerosene lamps lit the streets of Big Spring until the "Magic Lantern" arrived, Big Spring's first street light. (Malone Collection, Heritage Museum.)

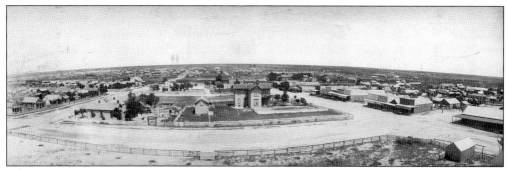

BIRDSEYE VIEW OF BIG SPRING. This photo was taken from the top of the Courthouse looking north. The street in the foreground is Third Street, which later became the Bankhead (Broadway of America) Highway. The large house in front belonged to railroad superintendent J.W. Ward. (Heritage Museum.)

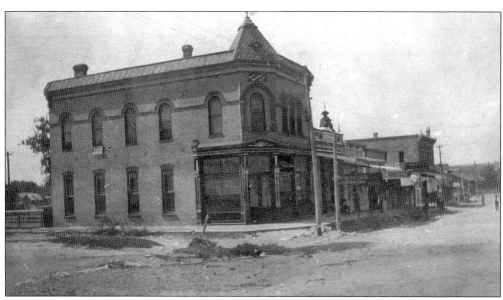

FIRST NATIONAL BANK. The First National Bank, chartered on April 19, 1890, was located on the Northwest corner of Second and Main Streets. The bank occupied the first floor of this two-story building, while the remaining space was rented to a variety of tenants. The post office was on the south side of the building until 1927. (Heritage Museum.)

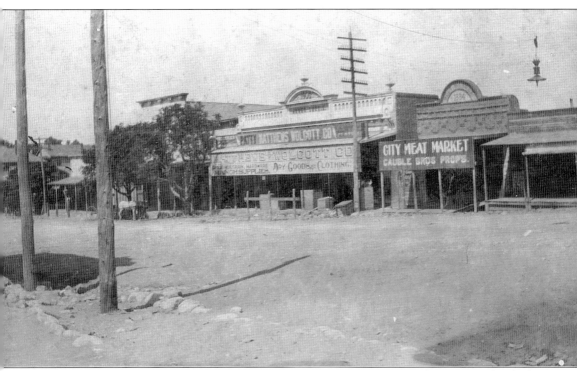

MEAT MARKET. One of the first permanent structures in Big Spring was the Meat Market built in 1884 by the Earl of Aylesford. Built at 121 Main, this allowed the Englishman to have mutton to suit his taste. Later, the Cauble Brothers became its proprietors. To the left of the Meat Market is the Patty Matthews Wolcott Dry Goods. This building, located at 117 Main Street, was built in 1900 by Rancher James Currie, and later became Big Spring Hardware. (Agnell Collection, Heritage Museum.)

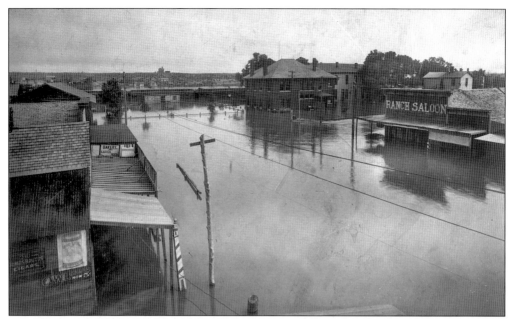

1902 FLOOD. In July 1902, after three days of flooding, the Sulpher Draw was converted into a roaring river half a mile wide. For many days after the rains stopped, boats were used to cross from the north and south sides of the railroad tracks. Stores and houses lining the blocks of First and Main Streets were completely ruined. (Pickle Collection, Heritage Museum.)

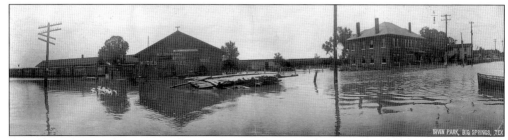

FLOODING AT RAILROAD. During the peak of the 1902 flood, water reached the windows of the railroad's passenger cars. People had to rely on boat transportation for three weeks after the flood. To prevent any future flooding of this magnitude, the railroad built a large dam west of town. (Heritage Museum.)

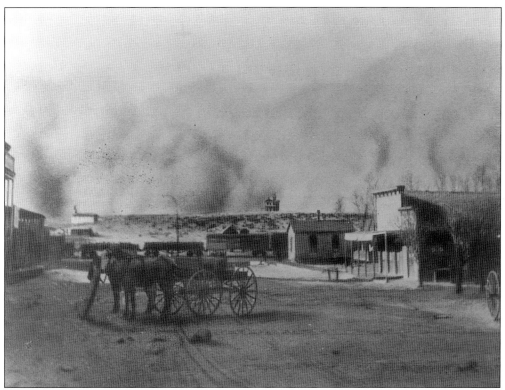

SANDSTORM IN BIG SPRING. On February 20, 1894, the sky blackened with a thick wall of blinding sand. People hid in dugouts and cellars, and newcomers thought it was the end of the world! (Alderman Collection, Heritage Museum.)

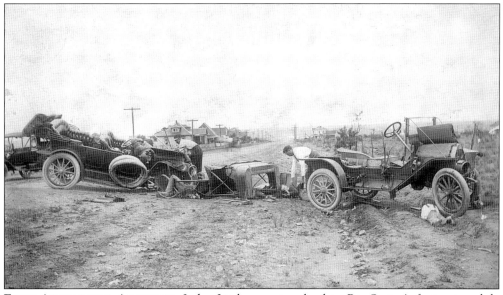

FIRST AUTOMOBILE ACCIDENT. Judge Littler was involved in Big Spring's first automobile accident at 1600 Scurry Street. The accident occurred June 17, 1913, with no recorded fatalities. (Heritage Museum.)

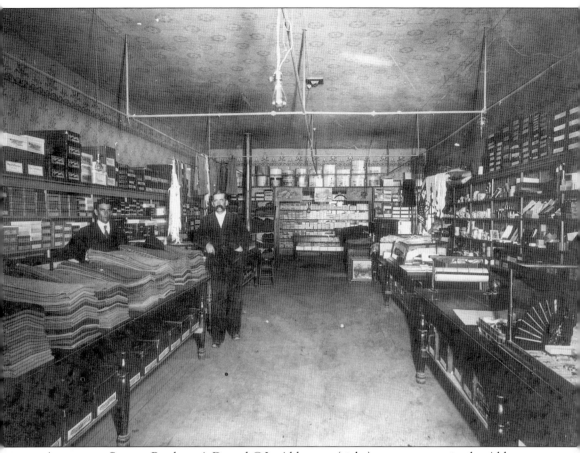

ALDERMAN STORE. Brothers A.D. and C.L. Alderman (right) were partners in the Alderman Home Union Mercantile Store. The store also served as Big Spring's first water department and telephone service under the ownership of the brothers. It was located at the southeast corner of Third and Main Streets. (Alderman Collection, Heritage Museum.)

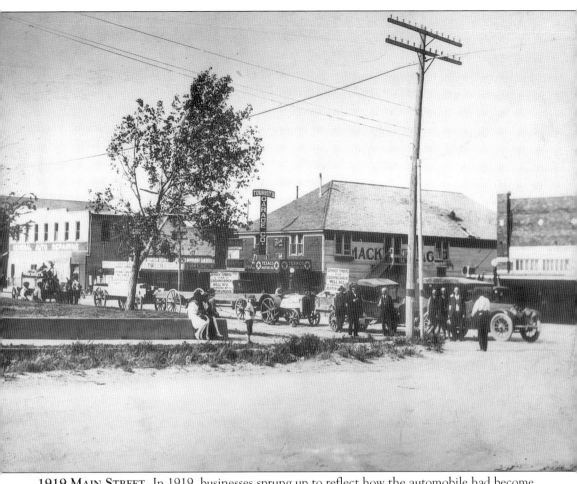

1919 MAIN STREET. In 1919, businesses sprung up to reflect how the automobile had become a new industry in Howard County. On Main Street, beside the courthouse, General Auto Repairing was located in the old Alderman Home Union Store location, and Texaco Tourist's Garage occupied the old Opera House. Stokes (Ford) Motor Company was on the corner of Main and Fourth Streets. (Stipp Collection, Heritage Museum.)

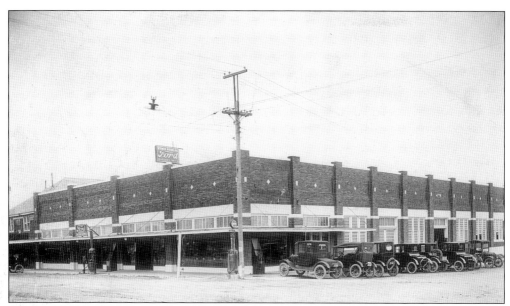

STOKES MOTOR COMPANY. The Stokes Ford Motor Company enticed many Howard County residents into buying a new Ford automobile. The gas pumps were located in front of the store on the corner of Main and Fourth Streets. (Bradshaw Collection, Heritage Museum.)

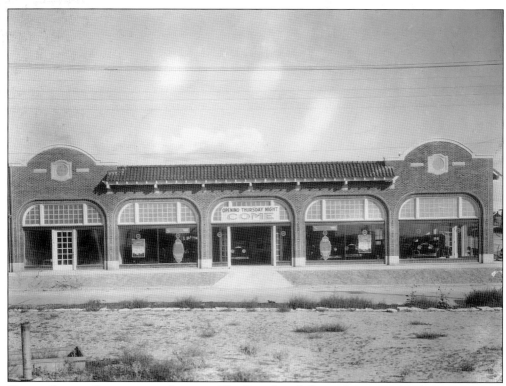

GREGG STREET STUDEBAKER AGENCY. The Fourth and Gregg Street Studebaker Agency was ready for their grand opening, featuring the $995 Dictator Model. The same building later became the McEwen Buick Dealership. (Robb Collection, Heritage Museum.)

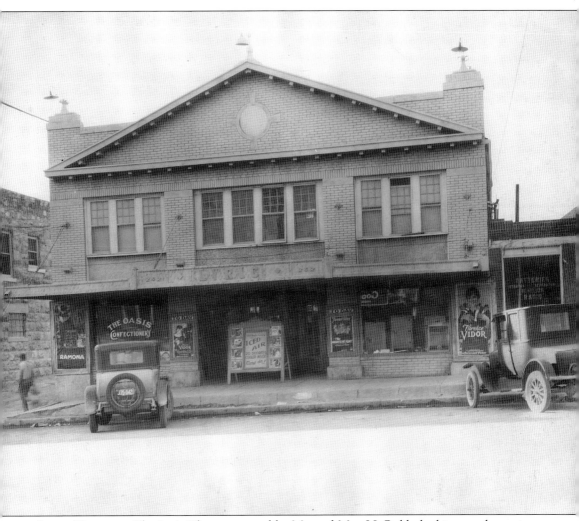

LYRIC THEATER. The Lyric Theater, owned by Mr. and Mrs. I.J. Robb, had its grand opening in 1912. The new theatre had a specially designed projection booth, and a buzzards' roost balcony. The Robb family was particularly proud of the French doors that opened with a push of a metal pole, giving what was then state of the art air conditioning. The Robbs closed the 110 East Third Street location in 1956. (Robb Collection, Heritage Museum.)

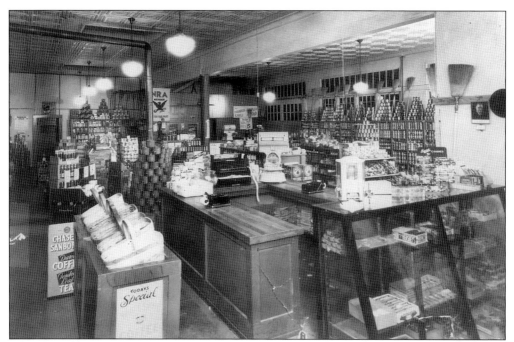

JOHN HODGES STORE. In 1933, John Hodge's store was located at 211 East Third Street. Canned goods were lined on the shelves to perfection and the new brooms were carefully displayed. Nickel candy was available at the candy counter. (Jordon Collection, Heritage Museum.)

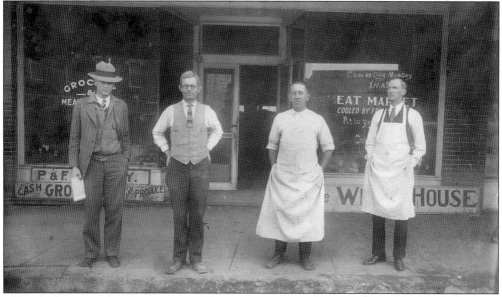

P&F CO. GROCERY. In 1926, J.B. Pickle and Victor H. Flewellen owned the P&F Co. Grocery. Later, Pickle formed a new partnership, changing the name to Whitehouse Grocery. The store was located at 1901 Scurry Street. Pictured here, left to right, are Hayes Stripling (salesman for H.O. Wooten Wholesale), clerks J.B. Gilmer and Andy Tucker, and meat cutter, Gus Pickle. (Heritage Museum.)

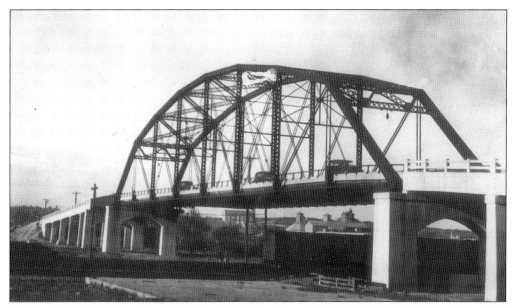

NEW BRIDGE. In May 1927, Melville, St. Landry Parish, Louisiana, experienced the worst spring flooding in recorded history, which caused the weakening bridge to fall into the Atchafalaya River. Part of it was recovered, and brought to Big Spring and used as the first overpass on Gregg Street (Hwy 87). (Pickle Collection, Heritage Museum.)

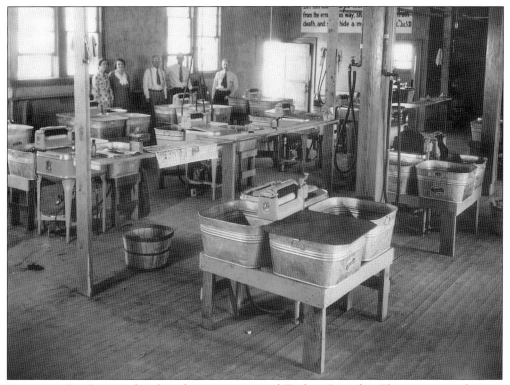

LAUNDRY. Big Spring's first laundromat was named Tuckers Laundry. They were proud to say all of their washing machines were Maytag. (James Collection, Heritage Museum.)

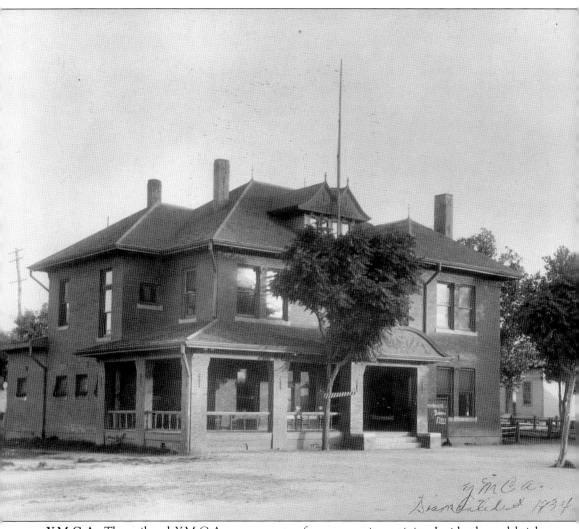

Y.M.C.A. The railroad Y.M.C.A. was a center for community activity. Inside the red brick building's downstairs area were game rooms, offices, a library, lobby, and tiled bathrooms with hot water showers. Meeting rooms and a large banquet area were located upstairs. The dedication of the new building was set for July 26, 1902, but had to be postponed due to the historic flood. The Y.M.C.A. was located at the corner of First and Main Streets. This beautiful building was torn down in 1934. (Bradshaw Collection, Heritage Museum.)

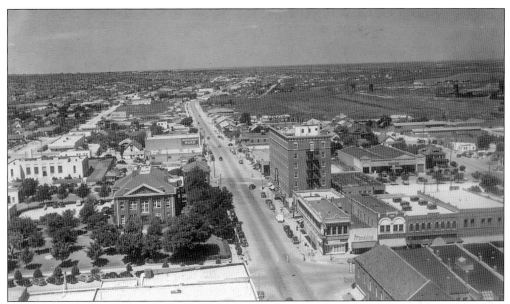

OVERVIEW OF BIG SPRING IN 1930. This is an overview of downtown Big Spring looking West on Third street, which was also known as the Old Bankhead Hwy. The sandstone courthouse is facing the Crawford Hotel. (Bradshaw Collection, Heritage Museum.)

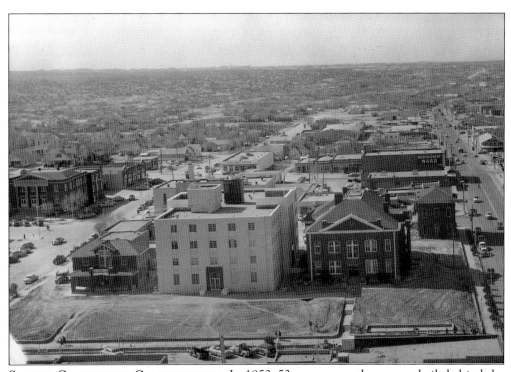

SECOND COURTHOUSE CONSTRUCTION. In 1952–53, a new courthouse was built behind the sandstone courthouse. The two story structure was no longer adequate and a new courthouse was needed to better house Howard County's justice system. (Heritage Museum.)

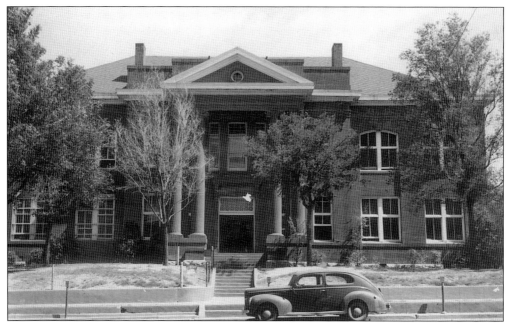

SANDSTONE COURTHOUSE. After the first (limestone) courthouse was declared an unsafe building, W.R. Cole purchased it for $3,084 and used the stones to build Cole Hotel. A new courthouse was built from sandstone, and cost a little over $45,000 to erect in 1908. The front of the courthouse faced North on Third Street. (Bradshaw Collection, Heritage Museum.)

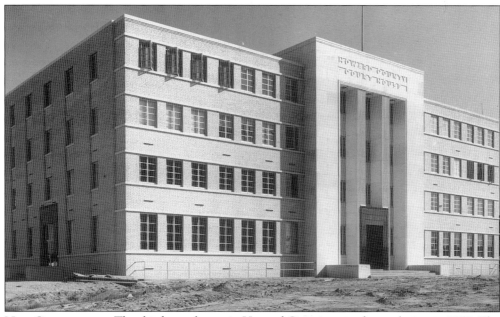

NEW COURTHOUSE. The third courthouse in Howard County neared completion in 1953. The brick structure has five levels, one of which is the basement. The new courthouse staff was thrilled to have more workspace. Several sections of county government occupy space as well as the sheriff's department and county jail. The courthouse is still in use today. (Heritage Museum.)

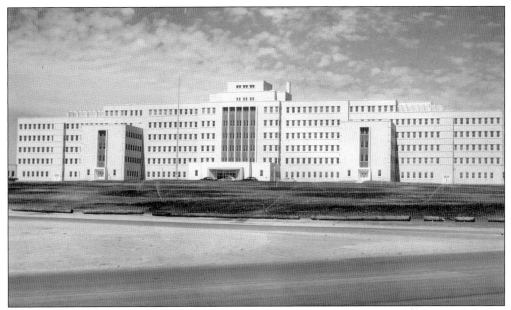

V.A. MEDICAL CENTER. Construction on the V.A. Medical Center Hospital began on February 2, 1948, and was completed on June 3, 1950. The main building consisted of six floors, a partial basement, and a penthouse. The building design included roof gardens for the nursing home patients. (Sims Collection, Heritage Museum.)

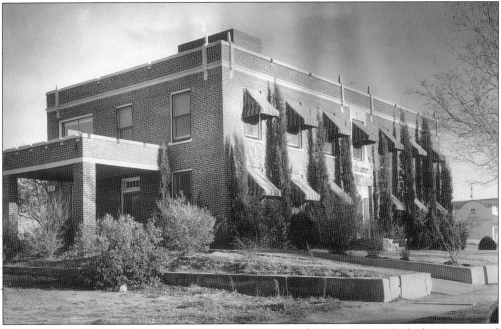

MALONE AND HOGAN HOSPITAL. Dr. Charles Bivings and Dr. Jim Barcus built the Bivings and Barcus Hospital in 1929. On November 1, 1938, Dr. J.E. Hogan and Dr. P.W. Malone bought the hospital. To decide whose name would appear first, the two doctors flipped a coin in the lobby of the Settles Hotel. Dr. Malone won the toss, and their new hospital was named Malone and Hogan. (Bradshaw Collection, Heritage Museum.)

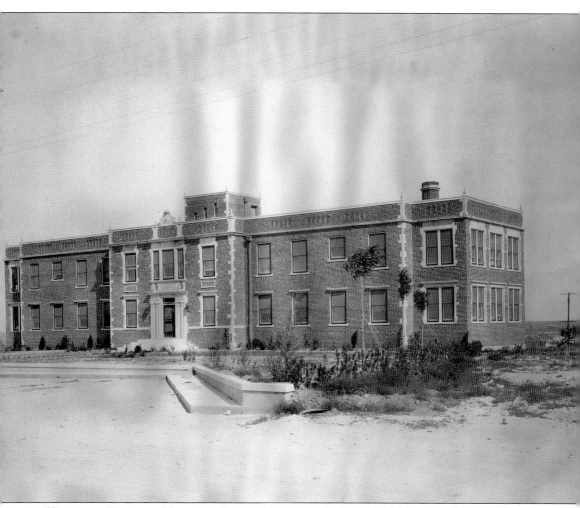

HALL AND BENNETT HOSPITAL. In 1928, Drs. G.T. Hall and M.H. Bennett built a red brick, two-story hospital at the corner of Goliad and East Ninth Streets and named it Big Spring Hospital. Dr. Hall went into partial retirement and in 1940, a new surgeon, Dr. Clyde Thomas, joined partnerships with Dr. Bennett. Dr. Bennett's daughter, Dr. Louise Bennett, joined the team as the new pediatrician. In honor of Drs. Hall and Bennett, the hospital became known as Hall Bennett Memorial Hospital and Clinic. (Bradshaw Collection, Heritage Museum.)

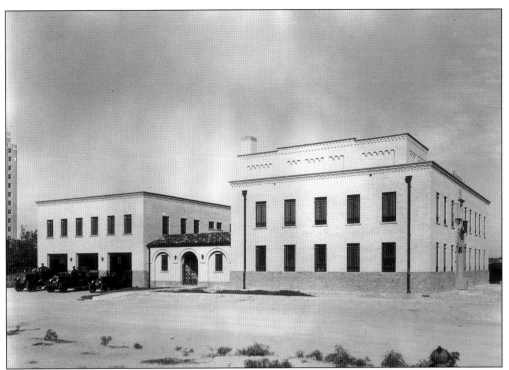

MUNICIPAL BUILDING. The Municipal Building was completed in 1932 after a $200,000 bond was issued for the project. The buildings two rear wings housed the fire department and the municipal offices. Above the fire department was the city jail, and located directly behind the building was the 1500 seat municipal auditorium. (Bradshaw Collection, Heritage Museum.)

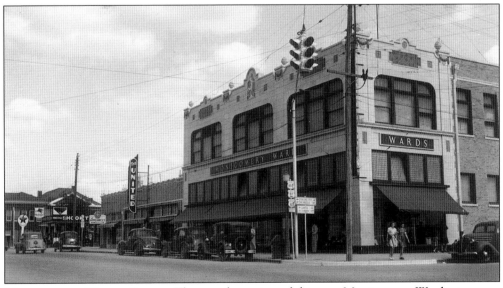

MONTGOMERY WARDS STORE. The grand opening of the new Montgomery Wards store was held on Saturday, May 12, 1935. Located on the southeast corner of Third and Gregg Streets, the store had a basement, main floor, second floor, and mezzanine. This photo was taken in 1941. (Weaver Collection, Heritage Museum.)

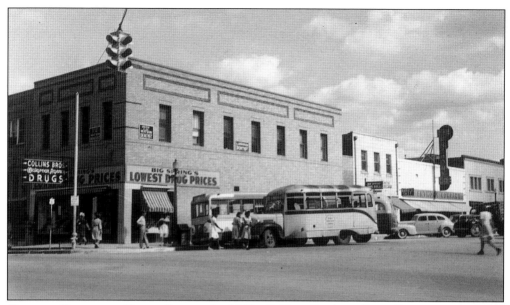

COLLINS BROTHERS DRUG STORE. In 1941, Collins Brothers Drug Store occupied this building, located at the southeast corner of Third and Main Streets. Also shown are the city buses, which were an available mode of transportation in the 1940s. (Weaver Collection, Heritage Museum.)

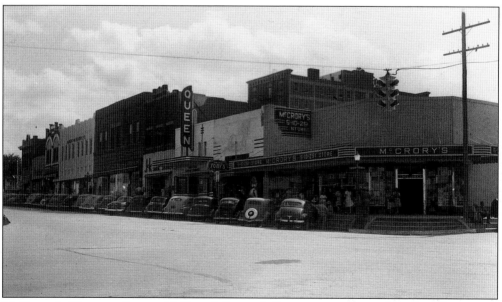

McCRORY'S VARIETY STORE. McCrory's five and dime store was located on the West corner of Second and Main Streets. Next to McCrory's was the Queen Movie Theatre, where many locals remember going on Saturday mornings and watching Roy Roger movies for a dime. (Weaver Collection, Heritage Museum.)

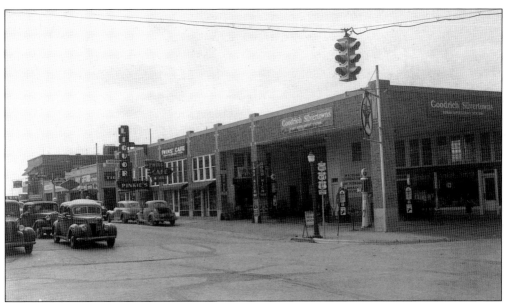

GOODRICH SERVICE STATION. Goodrich Service Station was located on the North side of Third and Scurry Street. Next to the station is the Twins' Café owned by twin brothers Lonnie and Leonard Coker. (Weaver Collection, Heritage Museum.)

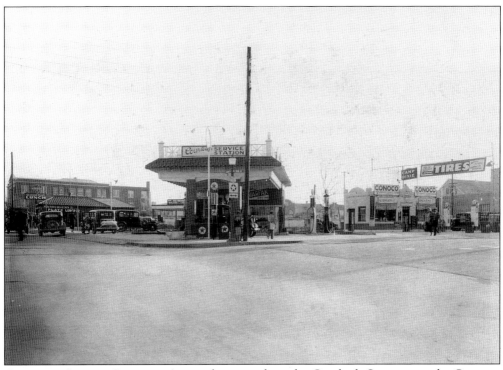

COURTESY SERVICE STATION. Across the street from the Goodrich Station was the Courtesy Service Station. It was on the South side of Third and Scurry Streets. To the west of the Courtesy Station was the Camp Dixie Conoco Station. (Bradshaw Collection, Heritage Museum.)

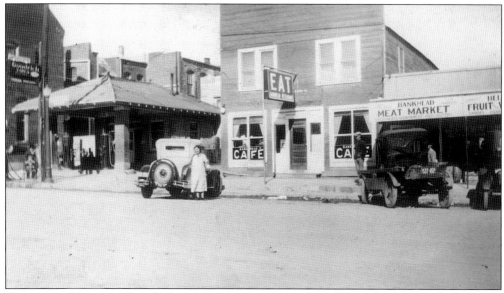

HOLMAN'S GARAGE. The Holman Garage was located on East Third Street behind the Masonic Lodge building. East Third was also known as the Bankhead Highway and businesses touted the name. Next to Holman's Garage were the Bankhead Café and the Bankhead Meat Market. (Bradshaw Collection, Heritage Museum.)

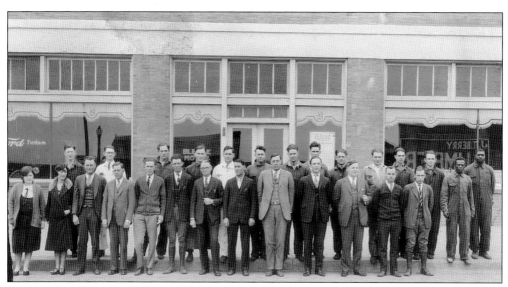

STOKES FORD MOTOR COMPANY. Workers pose for photographers in front of the Stokes Ford Motor Company on January 7, 1917. The dealership was located at the corner of Main and Fourth Streets. (Heritage Museum.)

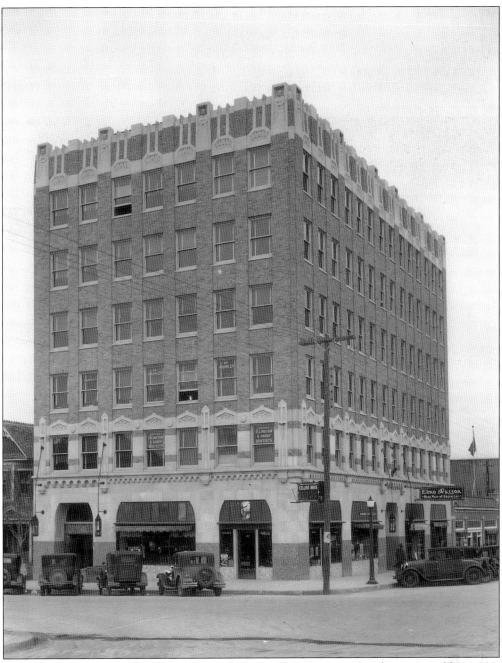

PETROLEUM BUILDING. In 1928, the Petroleum building was completed at a cost of $190,000. Ten precast, concrete Aztec warriors border the top of the building. A few features in the modern building were marble walls, brass accents, and a mail chute servicing all floors. The building was built to satisfy a growing demand for office space in Big Spring. Dr. Parmley and dentists Drs. Hardy and Ellington were first to rent space. Collins Brother's Drug and Elmo Wasson Men's Wear were also new tenants. In the 1950s, Cosden Refinery purchased the building, renaming it the Cosden Petroleum Building. (Bradshaw Collection, Heritage Museum.)

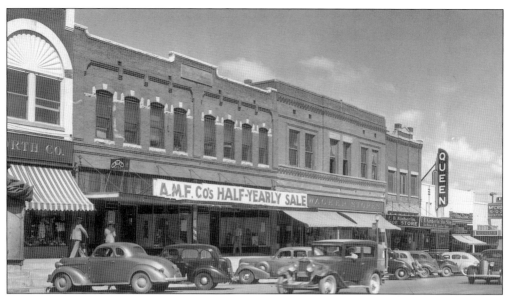

1940 MAIN STREET. In 1940, parking space in the downtown Big Spring area was hard to find. On Saturday mornings, vehicles were bumper to bumper on Main Street. L.B. Dudley, Woolworth, Wacker, and McCrory's were all five and dime stores located on the west side of Main Street along with the A.M.F. Department store, owned by Albert M. Fisher, and later sold to Hemphill Wells. (Bradshaw Collection, Heritage Museum.)

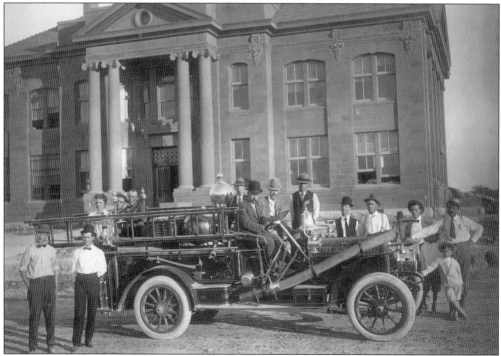

NEW FIRE TRUCK. Big Spring's new fire truck is parked in front of the Courthouse for the locals to admire. The fire truck arrived by rail in Big Spring on September 22, 1909. Fred McCrary was hired to drive the truck at $75 a month. (Heritage Museum.)

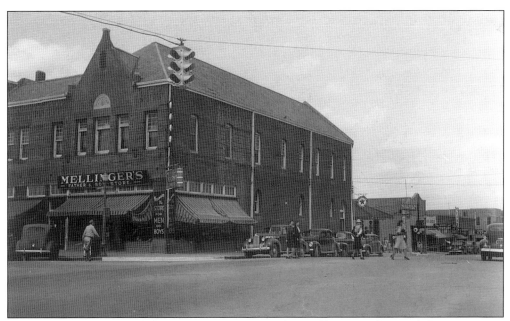

MELLINGER FATHER AND SON STORE. In 1941, the Mellinger Father and Son Store was located at the corner of East Third and Main Streets. Originally, Staked Plains Masonic Lodge built the two-story building in 1902, planning to use the top floor and renting out the ground floor. Their first tenant was the Western Windmill and Hardware Company. (Weaver Collection, Heritage Museum.)

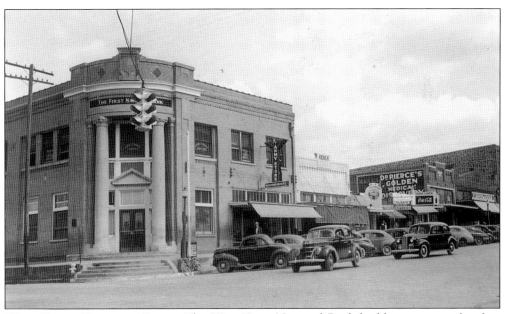

WEST TEXAS NATIONAL BANK. The West Texas National Bank building was completed in 1910. It was located on the Southeast corner of Second and Main Street. On February 2, 1934, it merged with First National Bank and became the First National Bank in Big Spring. On the second floor of the bank building, office space was rented to attorneys Clyde E. Thomas and R.H. Weaver, and Dentist Dr. Happel. (Weaver Collection, Heritage Museum.)

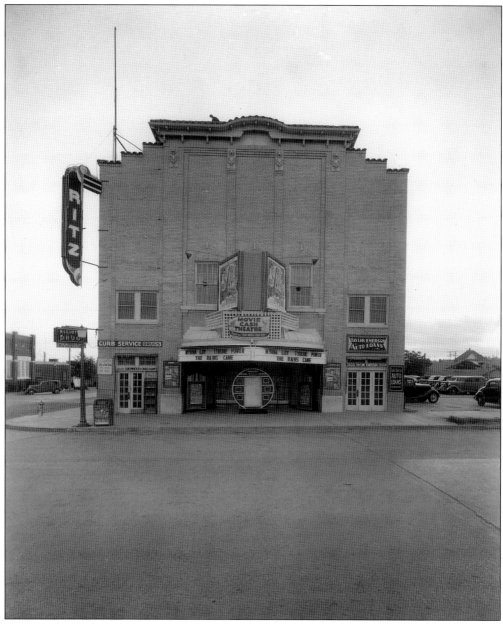

RITZ THEATRE. J. Yuill Robb and Ed Rowley built the Ritz Theatre in 1928. In addition to the movie theatre, office and store space was rented in the building. Tenants included Taylor Emerson Auto Loans and Elliot Drugs in 1940. (Bradshaw Collection, Heritage Museum.)

Two

LOCAL FOLKS

Many local folks contributed to the establishment of Big Spring and Howard County. A lot of hard work, sweat, and tears went into the making of the community as well as the development of each individual. Some of those pioneers left Big Spring to seek fame and fortune, and some left in a pine box, but each person left their mark on Howard County for future generations to admire and learn from.

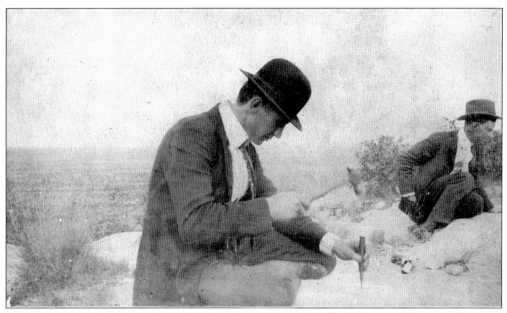

P.W. AGNELL. During a Labor Day picnic in 1902, P.W. Agnell (left) carved the initials "DKA and PWA" into a rock on the Scenic Mountain where they can still be seen today. P.W. and Della Russell were married on October 14, 1903. Tragically, P.W. was killed in a railroad accident, after only 8 years of marriage. Della was left to raise three small children alone. (Agnell-Hornaday collection, Heritage Museum)

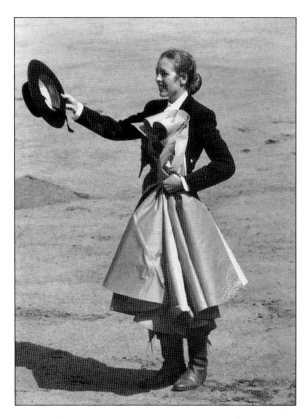

LADY BULLFIGHTER. Patricia McCormick is shown on location in Tijuana, Mexico, in 1953. Despite being tossed, rammed, and gored, Patricia was the only female bullfighter in the Matador's Union to hold top billing over a 10-year span. (Heritage Museum collection)

FRANK NORFLEET. Frank Norfleet developed a renowned reputation in 1919 after he was swindled out of $80,000. Norfleet, a rancher with a white mustache and trusting personality, was so successful in tracking down the swindlers that his services became in demand by other victims. He always carried a "thumb bustin" .38 caliber Colt revolver and was instrumental in the arrests of approximately 100 swindlers and the conviction of 87. (Bradshaw Collection, Heritage Museum.)

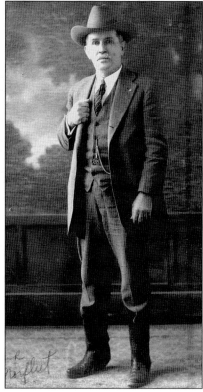

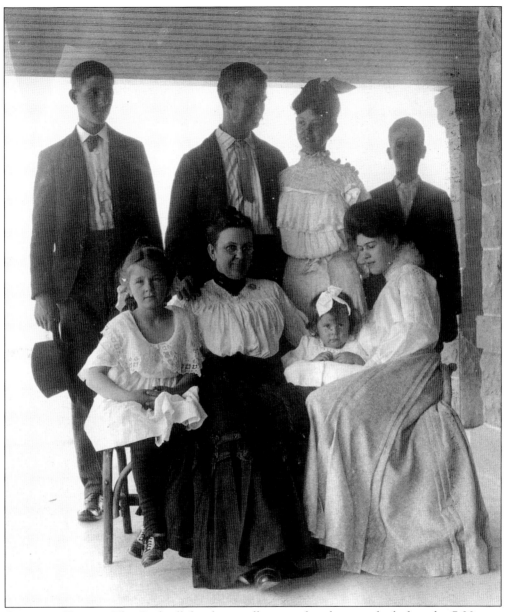

BIRDWELL FAMILY. The Birdwell family proudly poses for photographs before the 7:30 a.m. wedding of their daughter Lillian on June 21, 1904. Pictured here, from left to right, are: (front row) Maydell, Annabelle, Johnanna, and Lillian; (back row) Dan, John, Annabelle II, and Banton. The wedding ceremony was held at the Birdwell home also known as Redrock, and was the social event of 1904 in Big Spring. (Birdwell collection, Heritage Museum.)

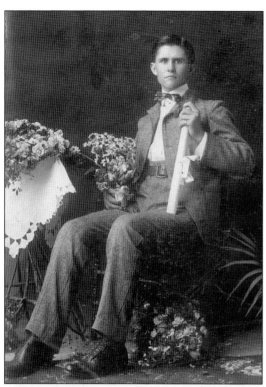

CLYDE THOMAS SR. The new principal, Professor Clyde Thomas, was pronounced "quite nice" by the young ladies of Big Spring. (Tibbs Collection, Heritage Museum.)

SHINE PHILLIPS AT PHARMACY. Shine Phillips stands at the counter of his pharmacy, Cunningham and Phillips. He used the scale in front of him to accurately weigh out the doctor's prescriptions. In 1942, Shine wrote a book titled *Big Spring a Casual Biography*, a book based on early frontier days in Big Spring. (Bradshaw collection, Heritage Museum.)

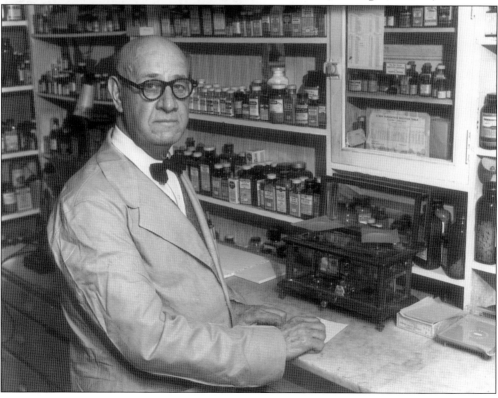

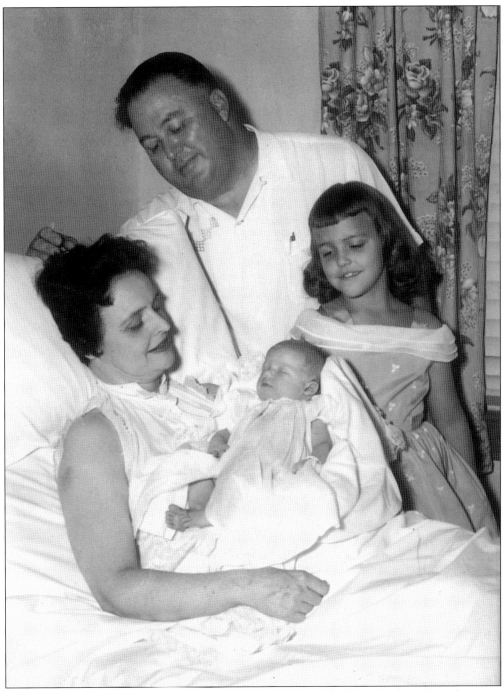

GARRETT FAMILY. Mr. and Mrs. Horace Garrett, along with their daughter Dorothy Ann, rejoice in the birth of daughter Melinda Sue. Horace was the grandson of pioneer Dora Griffin Roberts, and Mrs. Garrett was the daughter of Mr. and Mrs. Charles Dublin. Horace and Dorothy's marriage plans had to be delayed after Dorothy was diagnosed with a crippling case of polio that resulted in her being in the iron lung. On May 20, 1941, Dorothy and the "boy next door" were finally married. (Bradshaw collection, Heritage Museum.)

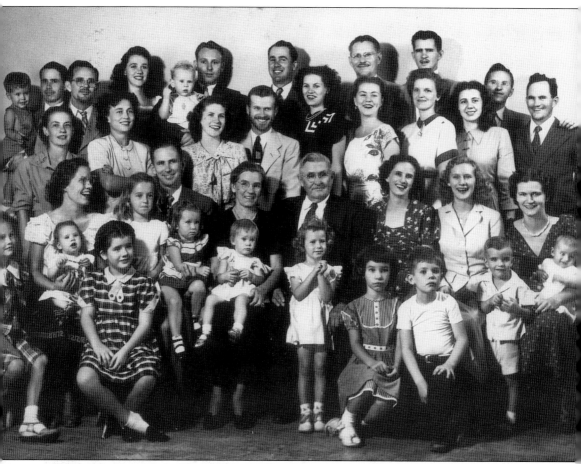

THOMAS FAMILY. Clyde Thomas met Reba while he was teaching at Central Ward School. They were married on June 28, 1911, and later Clyde returned to school as a student earning a law degree. He practiced law in Big Spring, and served two years as county attorney and two years as mayor. They had nine children, one of which was the beloved family physician to many local residents, Dr. Clyde Thomas Jr. He is pictured at the left of his mother and father. (Tibbs collection, Heritage Museum.)

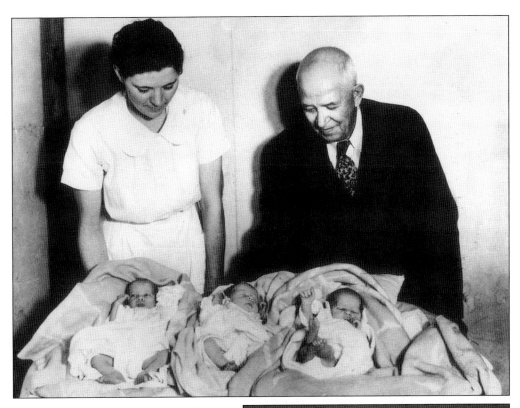

SHAW TRIPLETS. Dr. G.S. True and nurse Mrs. P.E. Little delivered the first triplets in Howard County. On September 30, 1936, the triplets were delivered in 45 minutes and were named in the order they arrived. Pictured left to right are Franklin, Delano, and Roosevelt Shaw of Knott, Texas. Dr. True asked permission to name the boys and did so in honor of the president. The babies were 12 hours old when this photograph was taken. (Shaw Collection, Heritage Museum.)

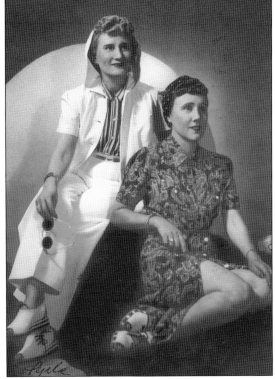

BRADSHAW SISTERS. Pyrle Bradshaw (pictured on the left) and Tot Sullivan (right) recorded 53 years of history for Howard County. The girls received their training from Midland photographer George W. Miller, and in 1922, opened their own studio. The pair lugged their Kodak 8x10 camera to notable points of interest. The Bradshaw sisters were experts at hand-tinting their portraits before color processing was perfected. (Bradshaw collection, Heritage Museum.)

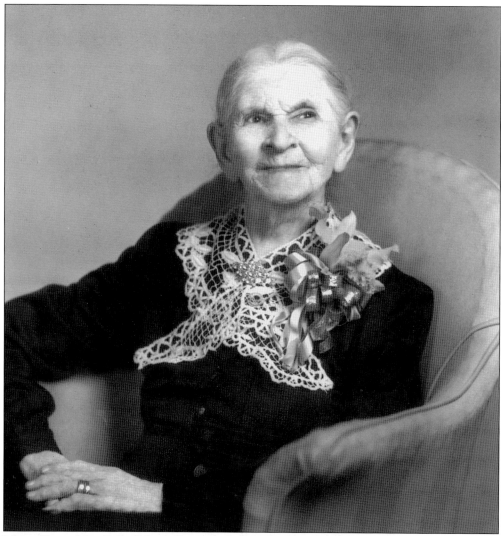

MARY ZINN. Mrs. R.B. (Mary) Zinn was honored with a birthday party at the First United Methodist Church. Mary was affectionately called Mother Zinn by most people. Mary and her husband R.B. arrived in Big Spring on April 1883 in a covered wagon. Mary said there were 13 saloons and 5 stores making up the business district in Big Spring. Cowboys would often ride through the streets shooting their guns in the air and running through her fence. Her son-in-law, Sheriff J.A. Baggett, tried to maintain law and order. Mary's home was on Scurry Street, where she lived to be over 100 years old. (Bradshaw Collection, Heritage Museum.)

JEAN PORTER. Jean Porter was described as a "little slip of a girl" that could give a bang-up performance that left most folks wanting more. She was a vocalist, ballet and tap dancer, and an acrobat. Jean went on to bigger fame and fortune as an adult when she signed with Metro-Goldwyn-Mayer in Hollywood. (Bradshaw Collection, Heritage Museum.)

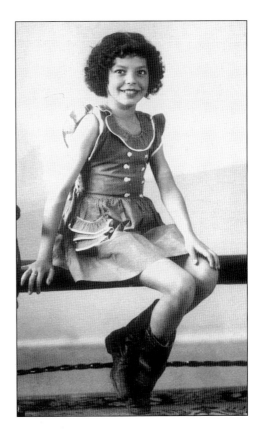

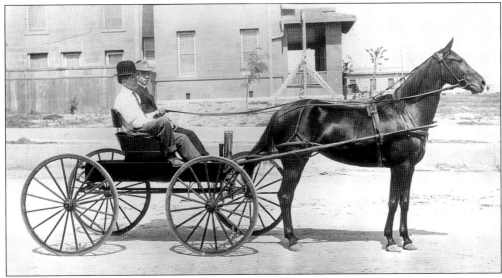

DR. ELLINGTON. Dr. E.O. Ellington (holding reins) arrived in Big Spring in January 1909. He and his wife had their "lovely" mare, Florence, and the buggy shipped to Big Spring from Henderson. Florence was part thoroughbred and Dr. Ellington would proudly race her. Dr. Ellington's dental practice was over J.D. Biles Drug Store on the corner of Main and Third Streets. (Heritage Museum.)

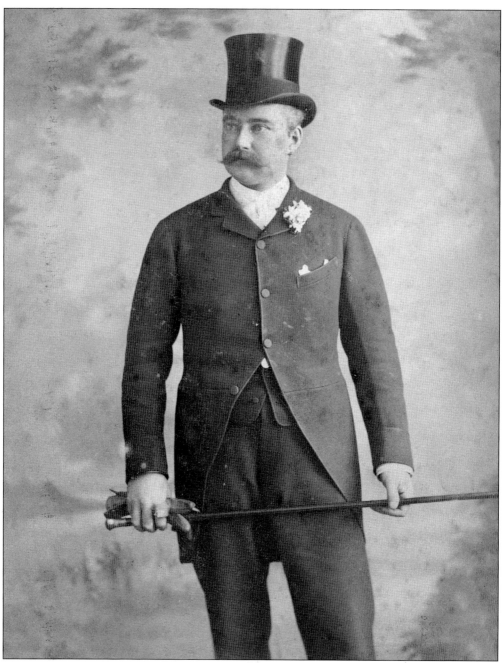

THE EARL OF AYLESFORD. The Earl dismounted from the train coach and announced his name to John Birdwell. "I am Joseph Heneage Finch, Earl of Aylesford, seventh member of my illustrious family to bear the title." John reputedly told him "That stuff won't go down here, we'll just call you 'Judge.'" The Earl arrived in Big Spring with his entourage in the summer of 1883. His passions were drinking and hunting, and in that respective order. On January 13, 1885, a card game took place in the Earls room. The Earl would rise occasionally to play a few hands. He stood up from the table one last time and declared: "Goodbye boys," and then he laid down, pulled the covers over him, and drifted into a peaceful death. (Heritage Museum.)

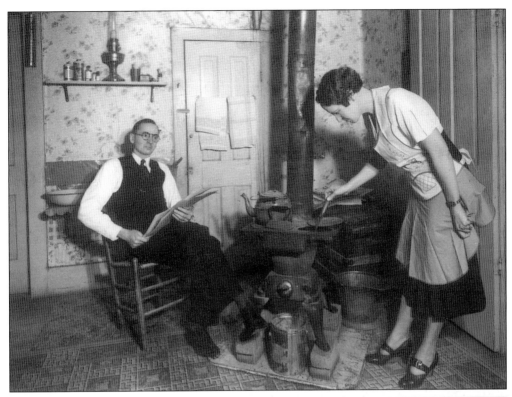

GRAY FAMILY IN KITCHEN. Mr. and Mrs. Gray are shown in the kitchen of their home in Sand Springs. Mr. Gray was superintendent of the school in the 1920s. The home was provided for them by the school district. (Bradshaw Collection, Heritage Museum.)

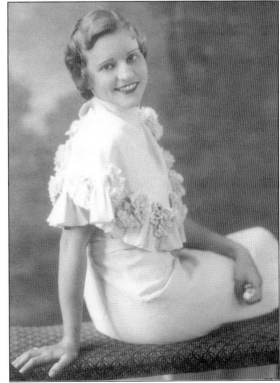

ZILLAH MAE FORD. Miss Zillah Mae Ford was voted Miss West Texas of 1933. (Bradshaw Collection, Heritage Museum.)

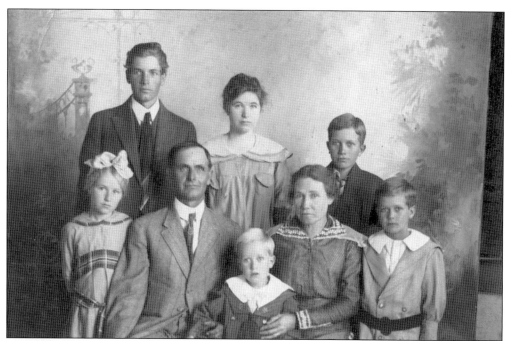

HAMBY FAMILY. Faber and Ellen Hamby moved to the Luther Community in 1921. They sold their Mercantile store in Arkansas and bought a large farm for raising cotton. Pictured here are, left to right: (bottom row) Lena, Faber, Jean, Ellen, and Vernon; (top row) Milos, Oma, and Dalton. (Courtesy of Nila Allan.)

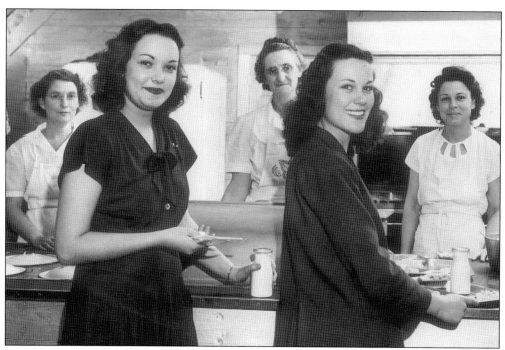

ACKERLY LUNCH ROOM. During the 1930s, workers in the Ackerly School lunchroom serve Kathleen Price and Hollie White. (Heritage Museum.)

Three

HOMES ON THE RANGE

The Webster's Dictionary defines a home as "an environment affording security and happiness." These homes were built with both characteristics in mind. Most pioneers started with very humble dwellings. Some lived in dugouts made in a hill of dirt, while others lived in a one-room shanty. Later, homes began to reflect their owner's successes, whether it was ranching, oil, business, or professional.

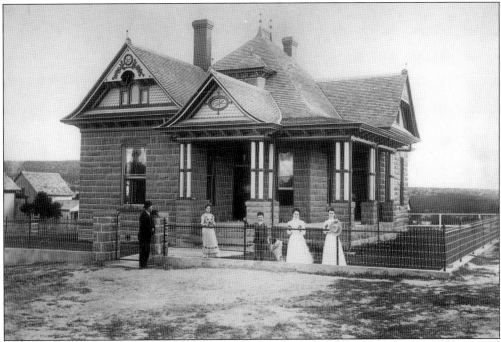

POTTON HOUSE. Mr. Joseph Potton, master mechanic for T&P Railroad, built the Potton house in 1901 as an investment and a retirement home. The Victorian home is constructed of 14-inch sandstone blocks and features a large porch that is supported with cast iron posts, believed to have been incorporated from the trains. The Potton's daughter (Mary Hayden) and her family moved into the home after her mother became ill. The Haydens lived in the house until their deaths in the 1960s. In 1977 the home was made into a historical tourist attraction. (Lomax Collection, Heritage Museum.)

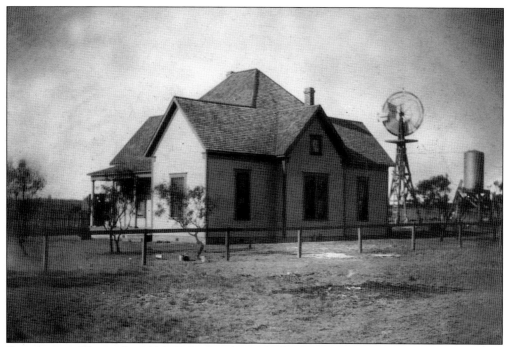

STRAYHORN HOME. In 1906, D.P. Strayhorn built this two-story white frame house, at 1600 Owens Street. (Heritage Museum.)

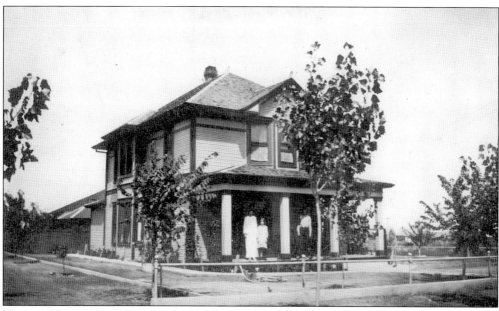

TALBOT HOME. Mr. C.E. Talbot built this home in 1910 at 1308 Scurry Street. Later, residents of the home, F.R. Weeg, added a rock addition to the front of the house, changing the overall look considerably. (Cook Collection, Heritage Museum.)

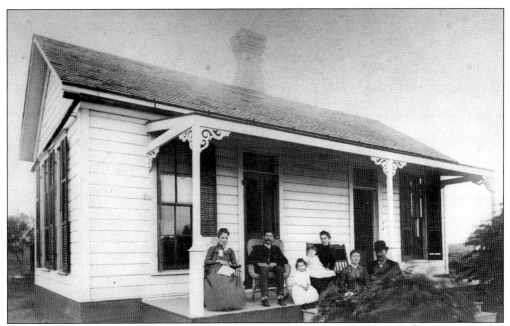

BRESSIE HOME. Milton Bressie, along with his brother and brother-in-law, owned the Bressie Bros. and Denmark. Milton and Mary Bressie's son Clarence Cherry Bressie was born in this home in June 1894. (Heritage Museum.)

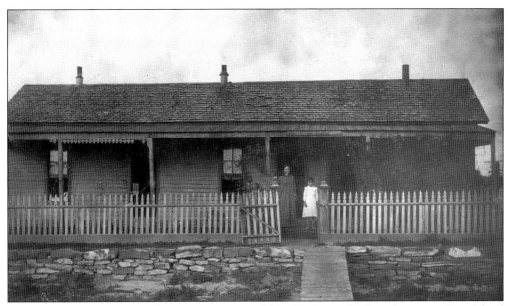

BARNETT HOME. Dr. Joseph Weir Barnett and his family made their home on East Third Street. The Cole Wagon Yard, (owned by Dr. Barnett's son-in-law) was diagonally across from the house. In the 1880s, lumber was scarce in Big Spring, leaving many of the early day homes without wooden floors. The dirt floor was swept daily with a brush broom. Dr. Barnett, one of the first physicians in Big Spring, arrived from Tennessee in the early 1880s. Proud of his heritage, every time Dr. Barnett heard the song "Dixie," he would take his hat off and throw it into the air. (Cole Collection, Heritage Museum.)

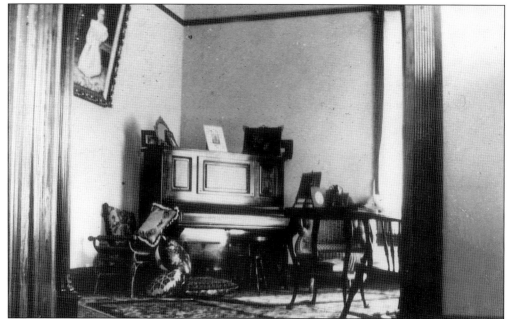

BRENNAND MUSIC ROOM. The music room inside the Brennand home was a source of pride. The moldings and woodwork were unique as well as the circular windows with mosaics of prism glass. Three massive fireplaces were always in full use during cold winter days. The H.W. Caylor painting "Little Willie," the Brennand's son, is shown on the wall to the left. William Jr. died of diphtheria at the age of 11. (Brennand Collection, Heritage Museum.)

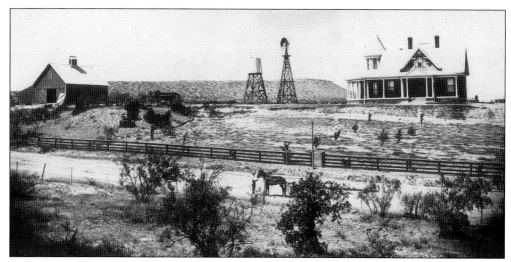

BRENNAND HOME. Mr. W.H. Brennand completed this lovely red brick home in 1901. It was built on 6.9 acres on what is now known as 1300 Lancaster. Double sliding doors allowed much of the home to be opened into one large room for social gatherings. Fifteen stately columns supported a wrap-around porch. Lush cottonwood and willow trees were planted behind the home and on the west side. There was a small playhouse for their daughter Annie Lou. Mr. Brennand raised registered cattle, and for a short time he operated the J.&W. Fisher Mercantile. They had two children while they lived in Big Spring, Willie and Annie Lou. (Brennand Collection, Heritage Museum.)

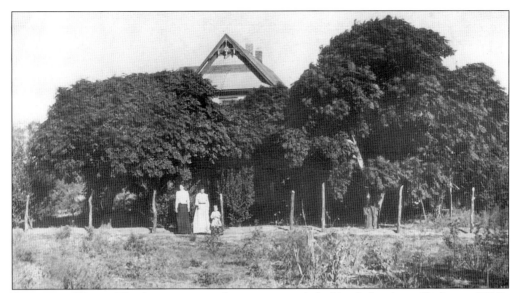

BOYDSTUN HOME. This large two-story home was nearly hidden behind a wall of trees. J.B.D. Boydstun built his home in 1882, after he had been hired by the railroad to run experiments in agricultural farming. He tested cotton, watermelon, tomatoes, peach, plum, apple, and umbrella china trees. An acrostic of Boydstun furnishes names for streets in the "Earl Addition," Benton, Owens, Young, Donley, State, Temperance, and Union. The city limits ended at that point so Mr. Boydstun never was able to use the "n" in his name. (Anderson Collection, Heritage Museum.)

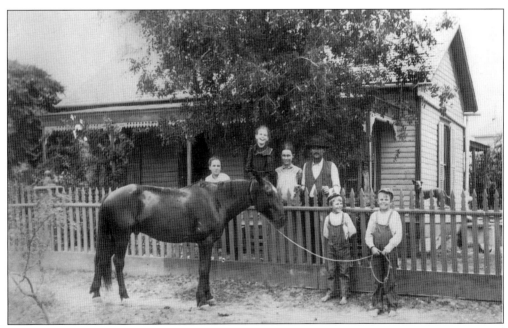

W.R. COLE'S HOME. In 1890, W.R. Cole's home was located at 308 Runnels. Mr. Cole married Dr. Barnett's daughter Sue. He owned the Cole Livery and Stable and later built the Cole Hotel. His family is shown here, from left to right: Pearl, Jo, wife Sue, and Will. Claude and Buster are standing in front of the fence. (Phillips Collection, Heritage Museum.)

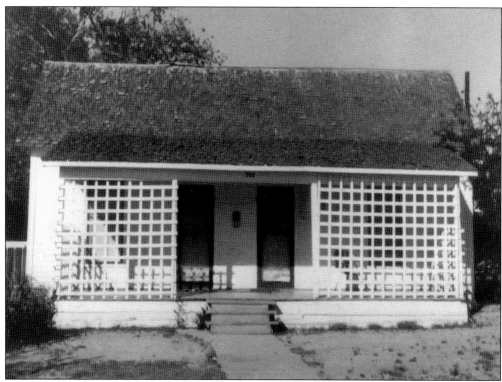

CAYLOR HOME. H.W. and Florence Caylor lived in this home at 711 Main after purchasing it on January 20, 1920, for $2,000. Mr. Caylor was a well-known pioneer artist. He painted hundreds of beautiful western art paintings. (Heritage Museum.)

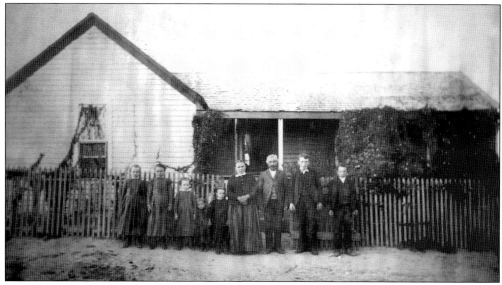

SCHOLTZ HOME. The Theodore Scholz family lined up in front of their home, which was located on N.W. Third Street across from the railroad shops. They are, from left to right, Helen, Thecla, Lucy, Carrie, Annie, Mrs. Anna Scholz, Mr. Theodore Scholz, Felix, and Tate. (Heritage Museum.)

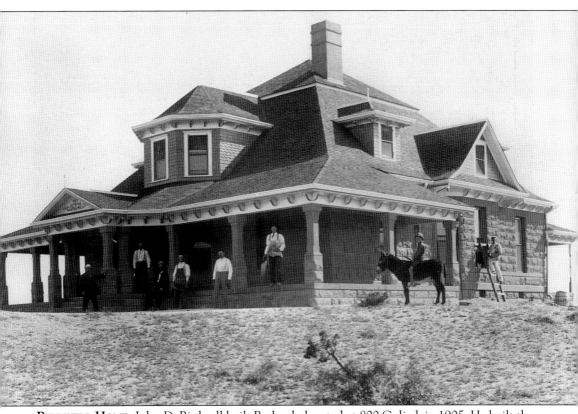

BIRDWELL HOME. John D. Birdwell built Redrock, located at 800 Goliad, in 1905. He built the home out of Pecos Sandstone, hoping it would be more structurally sound and safe from fire. John was once a Texas Ranger, saloon owner, sheriff, rancher, and later ran the T&P Hotel for the railroad. In the home were many of the treasured firearms John accumulated from buffalo hunters and frontiersmen, including a priceless set of engraved matching revolvers the Earl of Aylesford had given to him. The house had a large tank by it, which was often referred to as "Birdwell Lake." The Birdwell girls always volunteered Redrock for parties with their friends. John and his family had many happy times in the beautiful home. (Birdwell collection, Heritage Museum.)

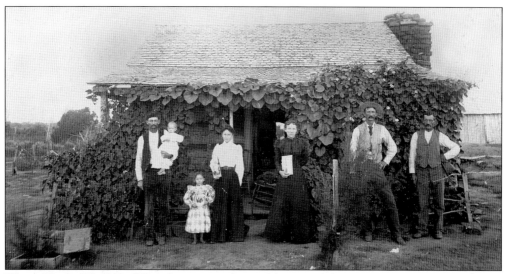

WADE HOME. The Isaac Wade home was a beautiful oasis on the West Texas prairie. The thick morning glory framed the front of the log cabin, which was built at the Moss Springs in 1898. Pictured here are, left to right, Isaac holding Mary Wade Hays, Brookie Wade Martin, Etta Wade, Belle Thompson Lee and her husband Bud Lee, and an unidentified friend. (Choate Collection, Heritage Museum.)

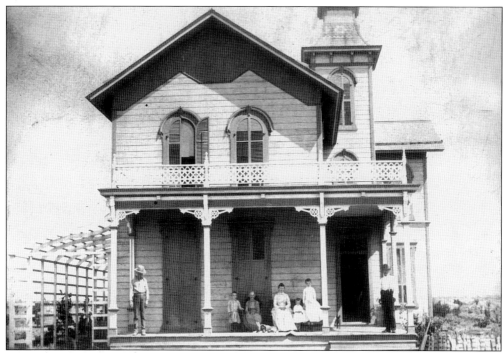

BAUER HOME. In 1895 the George Bauer home was one of the finest homes built in Big Spring. It sat high on a hill north of town and could be seen for miles. Mr. Bauer ran a saloon called Nip and Tuck. His home had features that reflected his occupation, including a barrel-stave fence. The house later fell victim to vandalism and was burned down in the 1930s. (Smith Collection, Heritage Museum.)

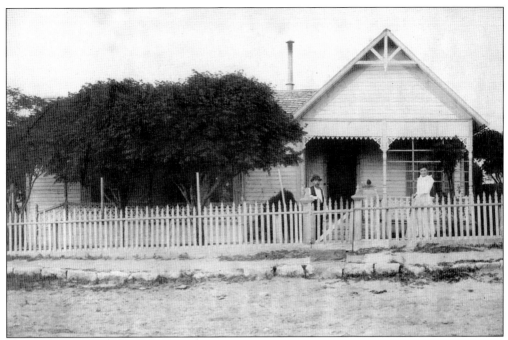

TAYLOR HOME. Aaron Yon Taylor was a supervisor at the T&P Railroad. He and his wife built their home in 1905 at 409 Scurry Street. His nickname "Yon" attributed to English idioms in his speech, "Lad, fetch me yon wrench." (Willis-Dawes collections, Heritage Museum.)

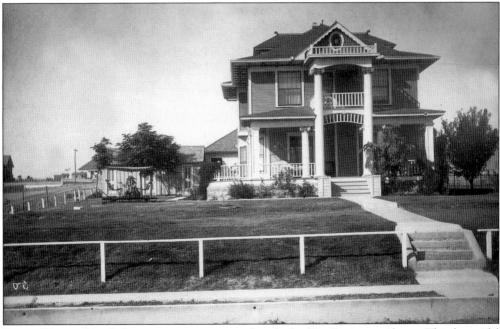

JONES HOME. Stately homes were a source of pride for Big Spring residents. This beautiful home was built around 1920 at 610 Scurry Street by Mr. and Mrs. Biney Jones. Later, Charlie and Anna Bell Eberley bought the home and built a funeral parlor in front. It was razed in the 1970s. (Atwell collection, Heritage Museum.)

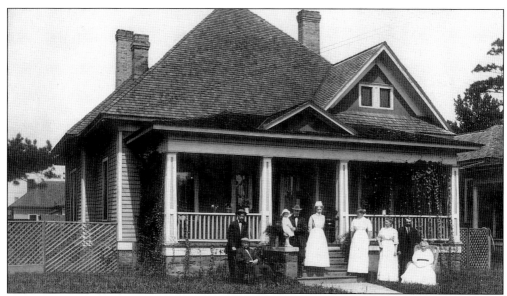

WRIGHT HOUSE. The first hospital in Big Spring was in this house located at 401 East Second Street. Dr. J.G. Wright and his "trained" nurses tended to snake bites, gun shot wounds, and all medical and surgical conditions. They would not admit "contagious diseases." (Wasson Collection, Heritage Museum.)

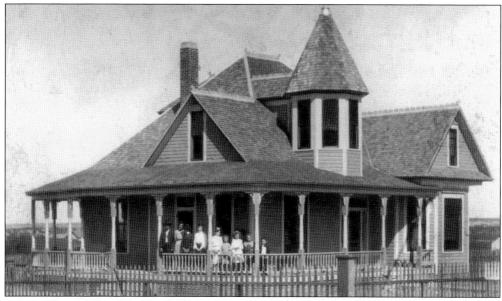

BROWN HOME. The G.L. (Bud) Brown home, located at 608 Aylesford, was built shortly after the turn of the century so the Brown's children would be able to attend school in town. The 11-room house was often subject to remodeling under the guidance of Mrs. Brown. Many changes were made, including tearing out the cupola that held the sewing room. The beautiful millwork, transoms, and staircase stayed intact. The family fondly remembers weddings, taffy pulls, and the famous fish fry. Mr. Brown caught an 80-pound catfish, and with no way to freeze it, he cooked it and invited at least half the town! Bud Brown was a rancher and co-founder of the West Texas National Bank in 1903. (Cauble Collection, Heritage Museum.)

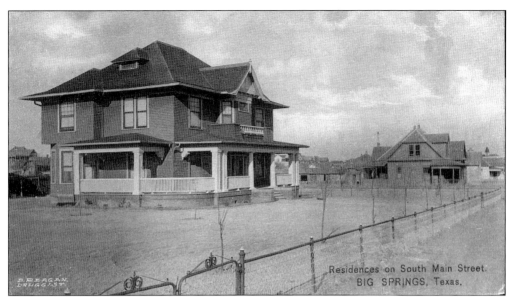

PRICE HOME. Ed Price built this elegant 15-room home at 800 Main. He chose this sight for its proximity to his work at the First National Bank where he served as president. Ed lived in the beautiful home for only two years before he passed away in 1908. Future owners made several changes to the home including a fireplace built in the living room. Later, another owner removed the fireplace and painted a mural in its place. The house originally had a stairway from the front entrance and the kitchen area, meeting at a landing just below the second floor and continuing three steps onto the next story. A coal furnace was used in the basement for heat. (Walker collection, Heritage Museum.)

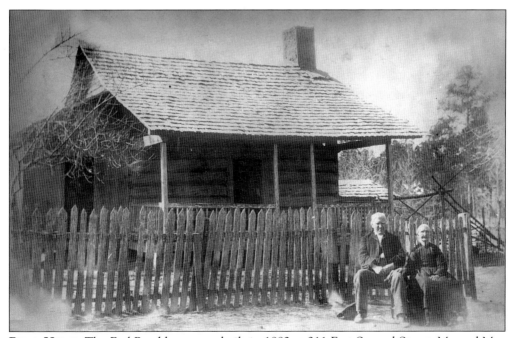

READ HOME. The Earl Read home was built in 1882 at 211 East Second Street. Mr. and Mrs. Earl Read are pictured here. (Read Collection, Heritage Museum.)

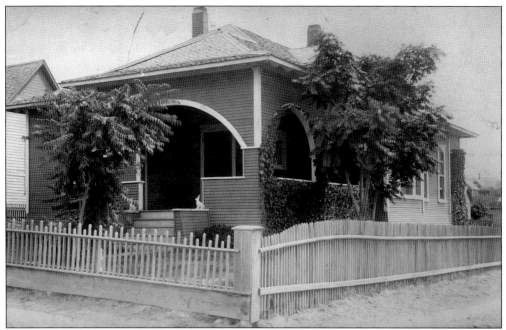

FISHER HOME. Albert Fisher was born September 17, 1885, to Joseph and Anna. He and his wife Edith resided in this home along with their son Edward at 500 Runnels Street. (Atwell Collection, Heritage Museum.)

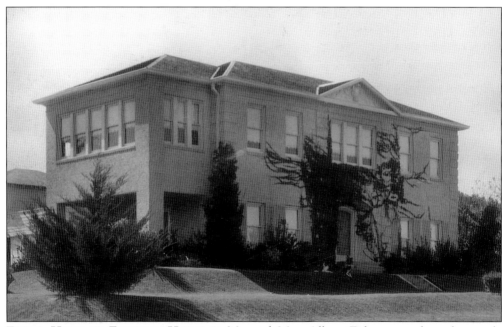

FISHER HOME IN EDWARDS HEIGHTS. Mr. and Mrs. Albert Fisher moved to the newly developed "Edwards Heights" in 1929. A photograph of the home was taken in 1939 by the Bradshaw Studios to be presented to Mrs. (Edith) Fisher as a gift from the Hyperion Club, where she had served as president. Albert owned and operated the Albert M. Fisher Department Store. (Bradshaw Collection, Heritage Museum.)

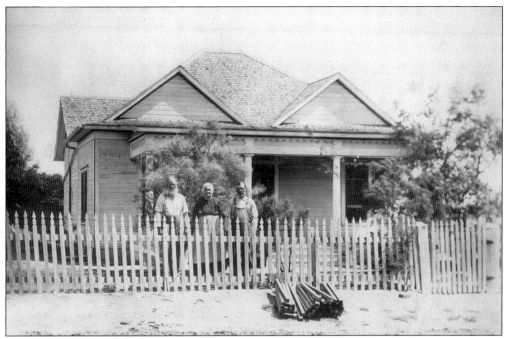

ROBINSON HOME. Mr. and Mrs. Charlie (C.J.) Robinson came to West Texas in a covered wagon in 1889. In 1902, C.J., along with his sons Charlie and Walter, bought adjoining tracts of land in the Midway community. The virgin soil had to be plowed with mules and a walking plow. Mr. and Mrs. C.J. Robinson and Robert Robinson are shown in photo. (Robinson Collection, Heritage Museum.)

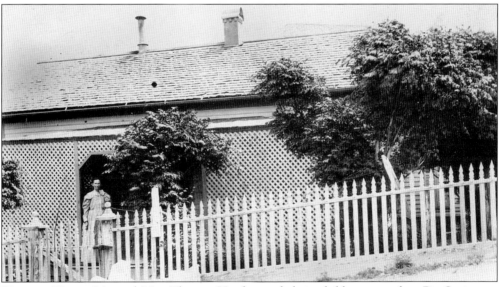

HAYDEN HOME. Mr. and Mrs. Thomas Hayden and their children moved to Big Spring on December 16, 1896. One of their sons, W.G. (Will) Hayden, co-founded the Big Spring Herald in 1904. Son Henry Hayden, a machinist for the railroad, married pioneer family member and neighbor, Mary Potton. The Thomas Hayden home was located at the corner of Gregg Street and 109 West Second Street. (Heritage Museum.)

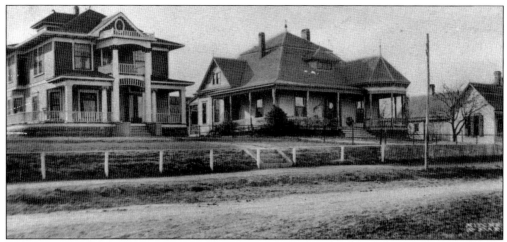

LITTLER HOME. John B. Littler came from Ohio in 1894 to practice law in Big Spring. He served as county attorney and county judge, and later helped organize and serve on the 11th Court of Civil Appeals. In 1900, Judge Littler built his home (right) at 608 Scurry next to the Biney Jones home. There was a beautiful balustrade on the front porch and the entry; at the front of the house were 10-foot double doors with heavy beveled glass windows. Ornate fireplaces were in the bedrooms and they had grooved and carved columns with beveled mirrors and tile facings. (Heritage Museum.)

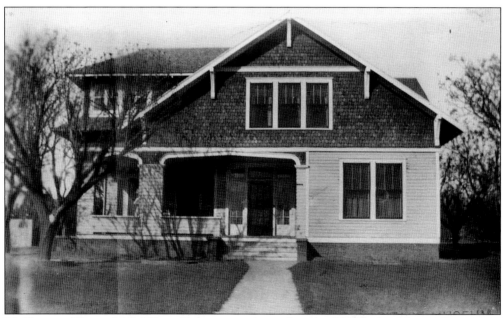

MCDOWELL HOME. J.I. McDowell's home was located in the 700 block of Scurry Street next to his brother L.S. McDowell. This area was known as the McDowell Heights. In 1941, Coy and Jessie Nalley bought and moved the home to 906 Gregg Street. It then became the Nalley and Pickle funeral home. (Heritage Museum.)

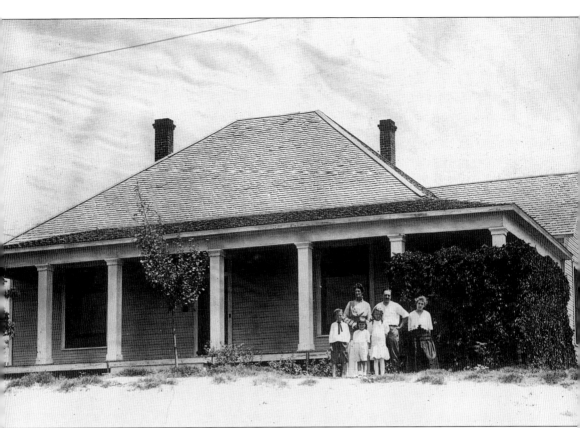

AGNELL HOME. When Pete and Della K. Agnell bought their home on October 8, 1908, she insisted that it be paid for before they moved in. This proved to be a very wise decision. A little less than two years later, Pete was killed in a tragic train accident, leaving Della alone to raise three children. The young widow, who had majored in Latin at Baylor University, opened a private school in her home for children. She tutored high school students on Latin in the evening, and would often coach railroad men in their correspondence courses. The 10-room home located at 311 North Sixth provided Della and her children with shelter and an income. (Agnell Collection, Heritage Museum.)

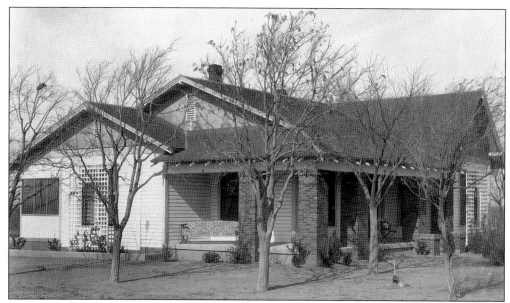

CAUBLE HOME. I.B. (Doc) Cauble and Mary Elizabeth built their home in 1905 on the Cauble Ranch one mile west of the Elbow school. Four of the nine Cauble children were born in the seven-room, white frame house. Brick columns replaced the wooden pillars on the porch during one of the major remodeling jobs that altered the look of the original home considerably. One of Mr. Cauble's daughters (Mrs. T. Willard Neel) inherited the house and still lives there. (Heritage Museum.)

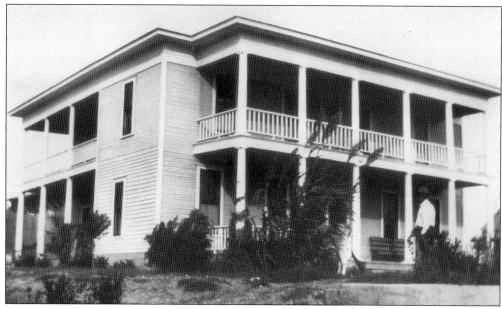

CARTER HOME. Joseph G. and Lillian Carter built this beautiful 10-room home in 1914 at 810 Gregg Street. Mr. Carter was a rancher and they needed a "town" home so they would be able to send their children to school. The photo shows Mr. Carter holding a harness to a cow. Daughter Ruth says, "Papa is getting help from our cow to clean Mama's flower beds." (Carter Collection, Heritage Museum.)

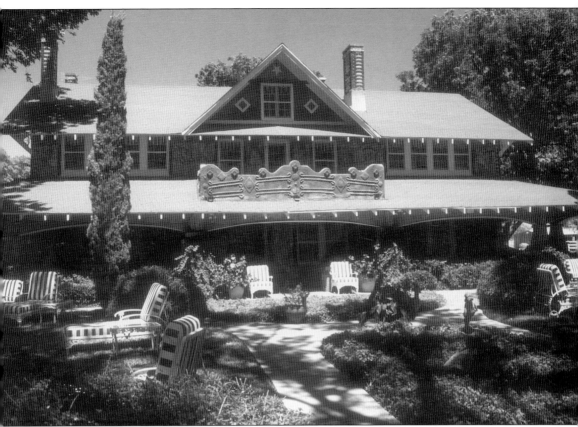

DORA ROBERTS HOME. The "House Of Rocks" is located in a beautiful valley deep into the Roberts ranch. Dora's love of west Texas rock inspired her to design a house that showcases rocks within the brickwork. The stones she most admired were set in cement around the main entrance forming a façade. Everything dear to Mrs. Roberts's heart went into the exterior of the house, from cattle brands to rope formations in the cement. Her most unique design is the evergreen vine formed of cement that winds over each of two gables into pots. (Heritage Museum.)

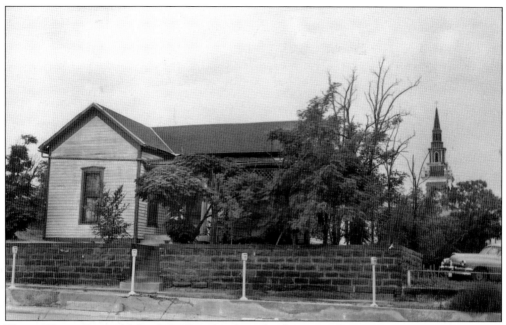

HURT HOME. Dr. and Mrs. J.H. Hurt lived in this home at the corner of Fourth and Main Streets. The courthouse was across the street on the south side of the house. The Hurts often used the water troughs at the courthouse to water their horse, Old Bill. Dr. J.H. Hurt was sent to Big Spring to be the official railroad physician. He performed delicate operations from removing steel from workmen's eyes to treating mangled arms and legs. Mrs. Hurt took care of the family finances by keeping them in a sock. She also kept very diligent records of the births that Dr. Hurt attended. Dr. Hurt was a physician to the railroad and local residents for over 50 years. (Heritage Museum.)

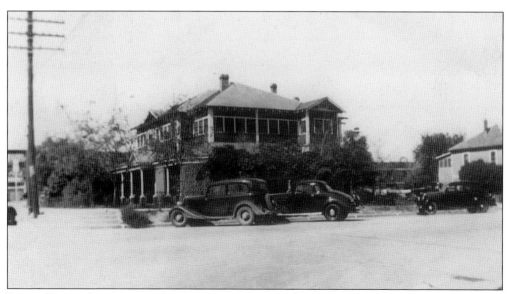

PENIX HOME. City attorney S.A. Penix's mansion had 21 rooms and 6 fireplaces. The home, located at 215 East Third, was torn down in 1939 to make room for a new gas station. (McDonald Collection, Heritage Museum.)

Four
LIFE ON THE RANCH

Cattlemen found thick grass awaiting them in most areas of Howard County, however the golden gleam of the grass soon faded to severe droughts and poor markets. Only the most stubborn and independent man could endure the hard and lonesome life of a rancher.

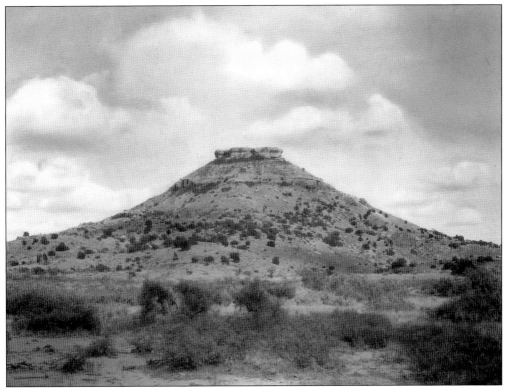

SIGNAL MOUNTAIN. Signal Mountain was once an Indian signal station. The Indians would build their fires at the highest point on the mountain to signal one another. It was said that the fires could be seen for a hundred miles in either direction. The early pioneers called the mountain Signal Mound or Beaded Mountain. Indian paintings and beads were found in large quantity during the early years. The mountain is located 10 miles southeast of Big Spring and is part of the Garrett Ranch. (Heritage Museum.)

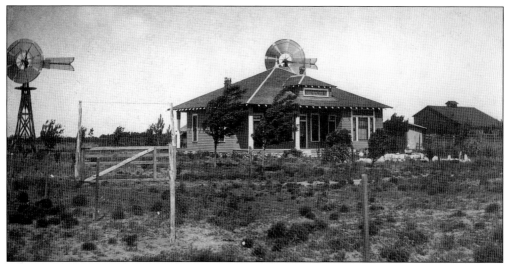

H.W. CAYLOR RANCH. The H.W. Caylor ranch was located southwest of Big Spring at Elbow. The home had two eclipse windmills and a well-stocked pond. H.W. Caylor was a local frontier western artist. (Heritage Museum.)

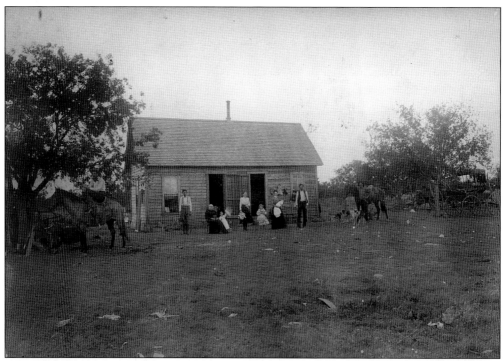

WADE FAMILY RANCH. The Wade family lived on this ranch in Howard County by Moss Springs. Pictured are, left to right: Johnny Taylor on horse, Jay Driver, Sallie and Mary Wade, Florence Driver, Brookie Wade, and Etta Roberts Wade, holding daughter Bertie. Next to Etta is her husband I.L. Wade. Mrs. Etta Wade was born to Mr. and Mrs. W.T. (Bud) Roberts. Etta and her family were the first permanent settlers of Howard County, arriving before the T&P Railroad. She remembered as a child hiding with her mother and the other children in caves fearing Indians. (Choate Collection, Heritage Museum.)

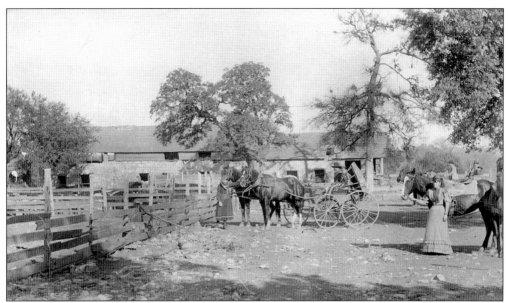

ROBERTS RANCH. W.T. (Bud) Roberts settled around Moss Springs in 1877. His dreams of ranch ownership were soon shattered when Will Wardell and Frank Biler bought the section of land containing Moss Springs from the State of Texas. Roberts waited until he brought his family to Big Spring before filing his homestead, which proved to be too late. The Roberts family was forced to move about a mile and half from the springs. He bought 12 sections from the state and secured grazing domain for his cattle. (Choate Collection, Heritage Museum.)

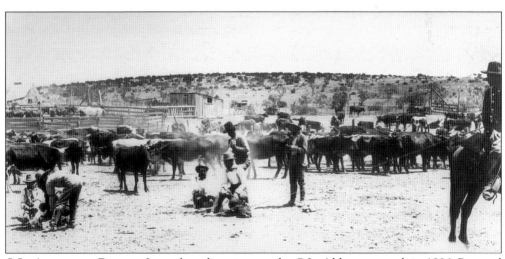

C.L. ALDERMAN RANCH. It was branding time on the C.L. Alderman ranch in 1886. Pictured in the photo are, left to right: "Freckie," George Cauble, C.L. Alderman, John White, Jim Donaghee, S. Alderman, and Bud Cauble on horse. Cowboys had to be quick and clever with their branding. If the brand was not used correctly, it would be slow to heal allowing flies to lay worms into the calves' flesh. (Alderman Collection, Heritage Museum.)

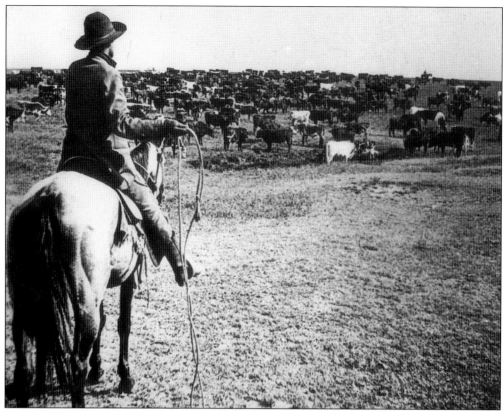

COWBOY FRANK JONES. Frank B. Jones Sr. watches over the herd, from the C.C. Slaughter's Long S. Ranch. The cattle graze as they move up the trail to Kansas. Frank was the last foreman on the Lazy S. Ranch. (Morgan Collection, Heritage Museum.)

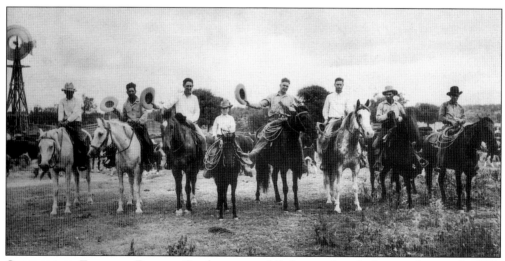

COWBOYS AT EDWARDS RANCH. Cowboys are saddled up and ready for round up at the W.P. Edwards ranch. On the left is the first eclipse windmill in Howard County. In 1884, ranchers would come for miles to see the modern wonder. Marion Edwards and his son, Sonny, are shown in center. (Edwards Collection, Heritage Museum.)

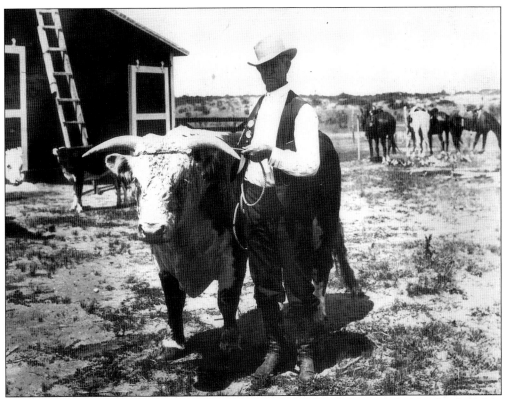

W.P. EDWARDS. Rancher and banker, W.P. Edwards, stands beside his prized white face bull. Mr. Edwards purchased the Lucien Wells Ranch. (Edwards Collection, Heritage Museum.)

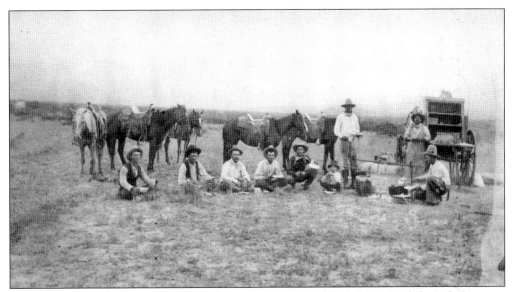

SHAKESPEAREAN COWBOY. In 1895, these cowboys were "Eatin' Out," while Rob Simpson (standing on left in white shirt) quoted Shakespeare. Cowboys liked to sit down by the campfire for after-dinner entertainment. Robert E. "Rob" Simpson, Shakespearean chuck-wagon cook, was always ready and available for poetry reciting. (Slaughter Collection, Heritage Museum.)

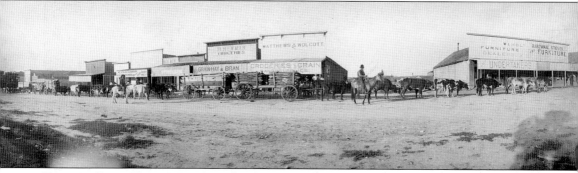

FAMOUS OXEN TEAMS. In 1896, the famous "Seven Yoke Oxen Teams" from the Long S. Slaughter Ranch are awaiting the command of "Uncle Billy" McWhortor. The two teams were combined into 17 yoke. They pulled a special wagon that was built in proportions to hold the entire cargo of a boxcar. "Uncle Billy" and his oxen team crossed over Benton Street to Second Street, turning down Main Street and swinging the teams into a "U" by talking to the oxen. After his supplies were loaded, Uncle Billy would drive the team back to the Slaughter ranch. It often took two weeks or longer to distribute the supplies over the ranch. (Stallings Collection, Heritage Museum.)

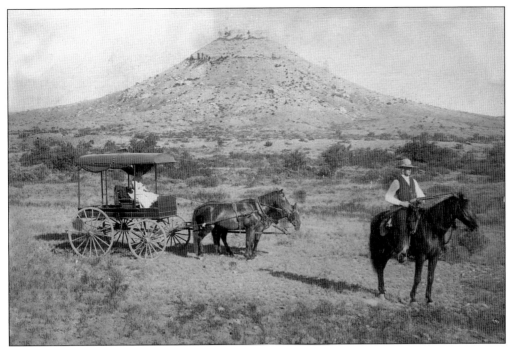

ROBERTS FAMILY IN FRONT OF SIGNAL MOUNTAIN. John Roberts came to Big Spring and joined his cousin W.T. Roberts in purchasing ranch land. John married the widowed Dora Griffin around 1900 and they combined their ranches. The Robert's ranch spread over 29 sections and included the Signal Mountain. After a fatal horse accident, John passed away September 28, 1909. Dora Griffin Roberts continued to successfully manage the ranch and oil business until her death in 1953. Arthur, son of W.T. (Bud) Roberts, is shown on horseback holding rifle. (Heritage Museum.)

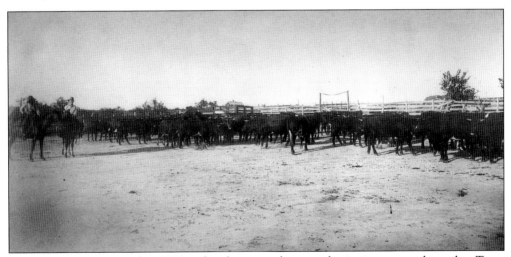

L.S. MCDOWELL. In the 1880s, shorthorn cattle were beginning to replace the Texas Longhorns. L.S. McDowell Sr. became the first shorthorn breeder in Howard and Glasscock counties. Mr. McDowell owned 51 sections of Glasscock County ranchland. The ranch still remains in the McDowell family and is overseen by L.S. McDowell III. (McDowell Collection, Heritage Museum.)

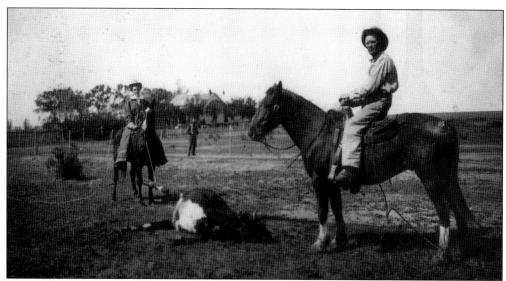

STERLING PRICE AND NIECE. Sterling Price and his niece Frankie Kent Tucker are roping a bull on the L.S. McDowell Ranch. Sterling was a dedicated and devoted cowboy on the McDowell Ranch for many years. (Tucker Collection, Heritage Museum.)

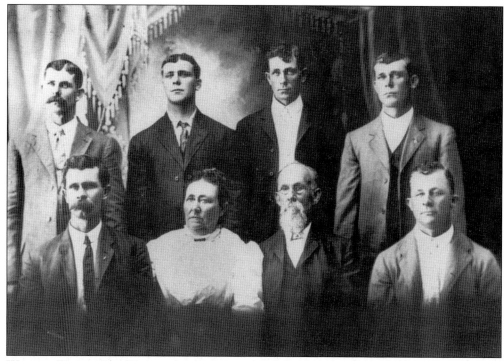

WASSON FAMILY. The Wassons were a pioneer ranch family rich in history. They owned several ranches in numerous states. A.L. was a rugged character whose career included fights with Indians, outlaws, droughts, crooks, and financial disaster. Pictured here are: (front row) Arthur Lee, Mrs. C.L. (Harriet) Wasson, Mr. Columbus Lee Wasson, and Claude Loraine; (back row) James Wiley, Craven Adair, Ira Elmo, and Sidney Earl. (Courtesy of Mr. and Mrs. Robert Ragan.)

Five

RAILROAD

The railroad was pushed westward by Jay Gould, president of T&P and arrived in Big Spring on May 28, 1881. "The 'Iron Horse' opened the West to settlement and development in the 19th century."

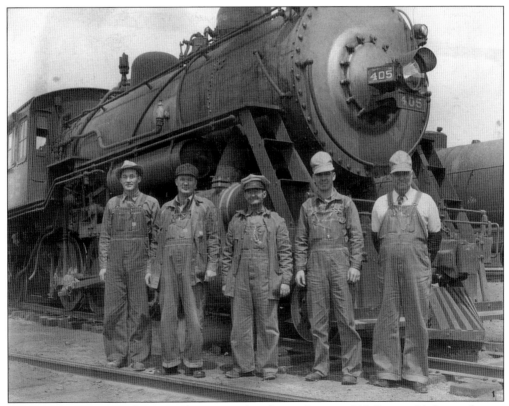

ENGINE 405. In 1943, these switchmen stand in front of engine 405. Pictured left to right are: switchmen Gibbs and Charlie Smith, unidentified gentleman, fireman W.H. Bain, and engineer John Smith. (Heritage Museum.)

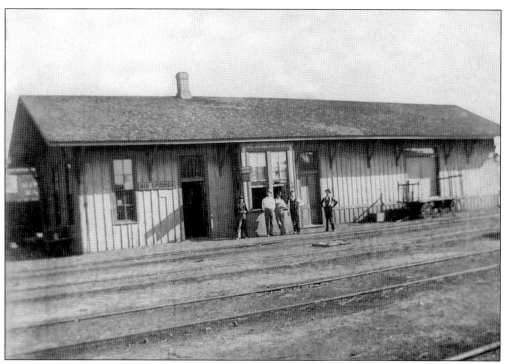

T&P DEPOT. The T&P Depot was built before the first train arrived in 1881. It housed the ticket office, passengers, and all types of freight. In 1903, Big Spring's leading employer and number one industry was the railroad. (Dobbins Collection, Heritage Museum.)

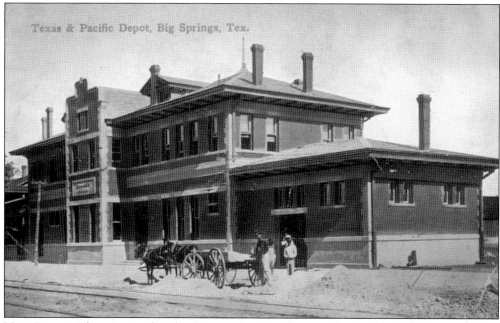

NEW DEPOT. Thirty years after the first wooden depot was erected, a new building went up in its place. The new building signified the staying power of the railroad and was a more permanent structure made of brick and stone. It was completed in 1910. (Heritage Museum.)

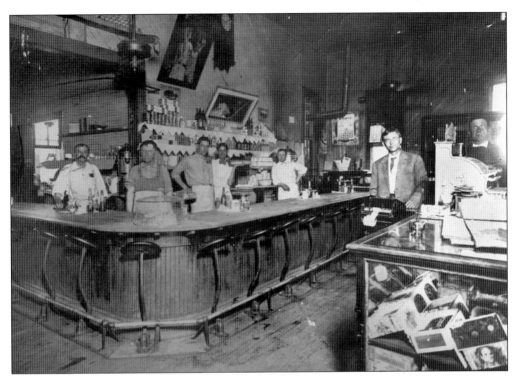

RAILROAD CAFÉ. Built in 1882, the Railroad Café was a popular eating-place. It was open around the clock for passengers and railroad employees. It was sold to J.C. Horn who operated it as a restaurant and soda fountain for several years. (Heritage Museum.)

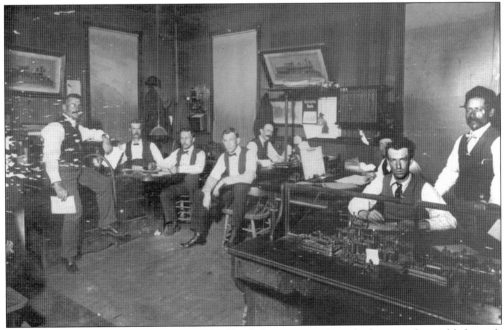

TELEGRAPHERS. T&P telegraphers and officials kept in touch with the outside world through the clickety-clack of the key and a Prince Albert Tobacco can. (Heritage Museum.)

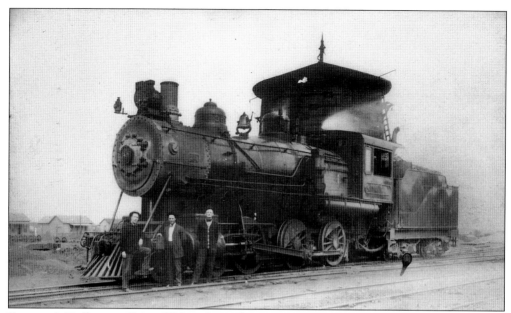

ENGINE 369. Boomer Dean, Walter C. Bird, and Dave Mims are standing in front of Engine 369. (Cowden Collection, Heritage Museum.)

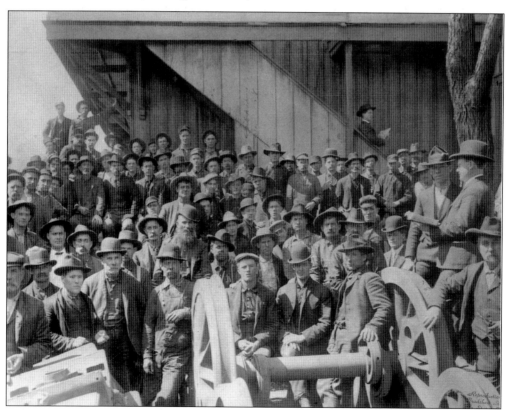

PREACHER AT SHOPS. In 1905, a Methodist minister preached to the workers at the T&P shops. (Heritage Museum.)

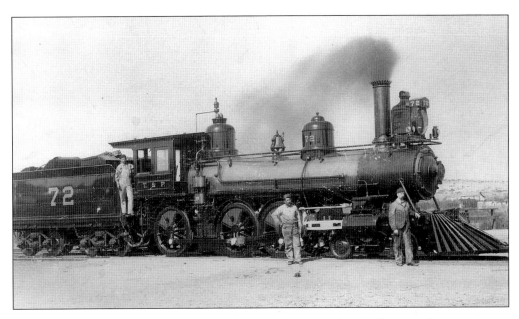

TWO TRAIN ACCIDENTS. Accidents were aplenty with the railroad. The steam locomotive was sometimes known as a "mobile bomb." When the boilers ran dry, the crown block would rip and the locomotive would explode. The engine crew was killed not only from the detonation but also from the heated steam. In the early 1900s these two trains had a head on collision. (Cowden Collection, Heritage Museum.)

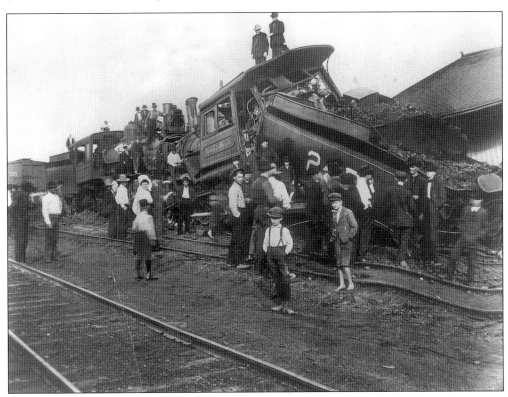

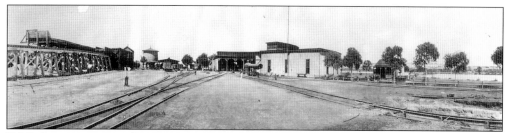

T&P ROUNDHOUSE. This T&P Roundhouse was built in 1881 and then destroyed by fire in 1886. A stockyard was located on one side of the tracks and a large body of water was on the opposite side. Swampy, unhealthy working conditions endangered the railroad employee's health. In 1929, one of the biggest jobs the railroad had ever undertaken was the construction of new railroad shops and a 23-stall roundhouse. A more suitable site was selected several hundred yards west from the old shops. (Currie Collection, Heritage Museum.)

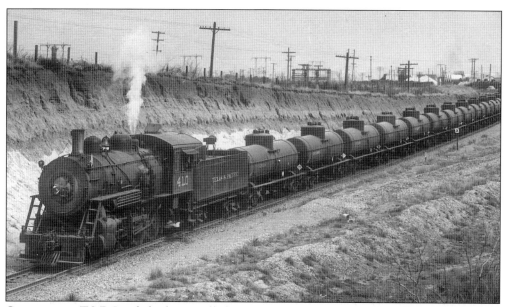

COSDEN AND T&P. Loaded oil cars pulled away from Cosden's refinery in February 1947. The locomotive engine 410 was called a "pipeline on wheels." Cosden and T&P Railroad's combined effort delivered thousands of barrels of refined petroleum throughout the nation. (Bradshaw collection, Heritage Museum.)

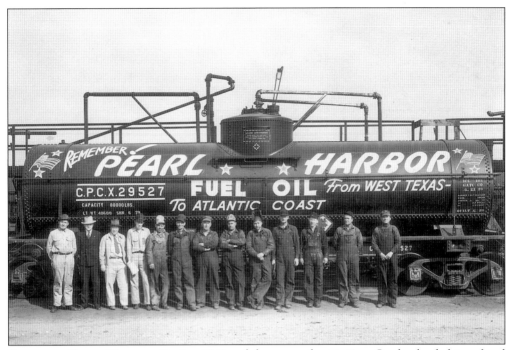

REMEMBER PEARL HARBOR. During 1942 and the wave of patriotism, Cosden loaded its refined oil into cars with the words "Remember Pearl Harbor" painted on the sides. (Bradshaw Collection, Heritage Museum.)

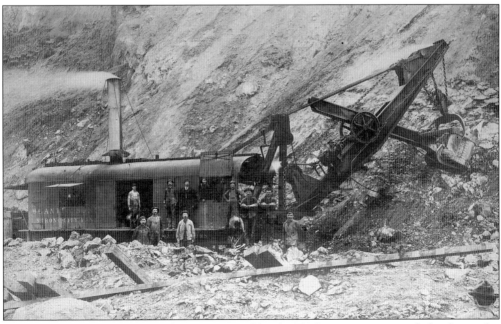

EXCAVATING MACHINERY. Machinery was used by the T&P to excavate a path for the tracks. In 1892 the T&P replaced its first rugged tracks with 56-pound steel rails imported from England. After several grade improved tracks were replaced through the years, a 110-pound rail was installed in 1932. (Phillips Collection, Heritage Museum.)

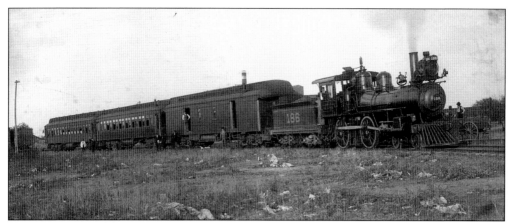

EARLY DAY TRAIN SERVICE. Train service was established on a regular basis on May 28, 1881, in Big Spring. The crude wooden and drafty cars leaked and creaked. Cast iron stoves gave off heat, kerosene lanterns provided light, and the seats were fashioned out of narrow, varnished shiplap. Despite the primitive conditions, travelers were thrilled to ride across the country at 30 to 35 miles per hour! (Heritage Museum.)

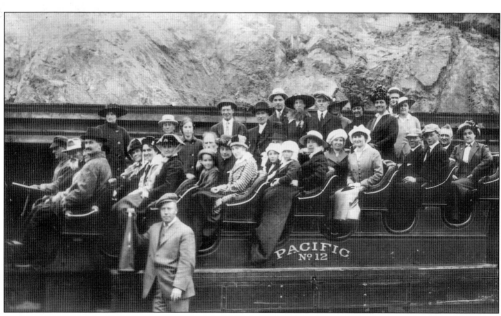

RAILWAY BUS. The Texas and Pacific Railway bus was used to carry prospective landowners to sale sites offered by the T&P Company through land agents. (Carter Collection, Heritage Museum.)

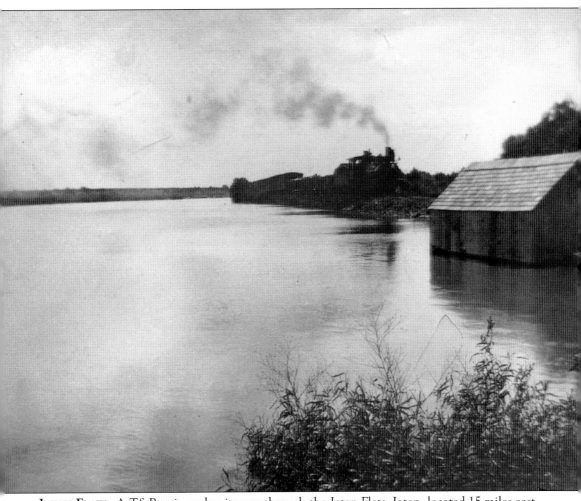

IATAN FLATS. A T&P train makes its way through the Iatan Flats. Iatan, located 15 miles east of Big Spring, was a favorite location for the youth to have picnics and swim in the lake. Iatan was originally named Satan Flats, but due to an error made during translation, the 'S' was incorrectly removed and an 'I' was put in its place. The reason it was initially given the name "Satan Flats" was because "the roads were hell on wheeled vehicles." (Heritage Museum.)

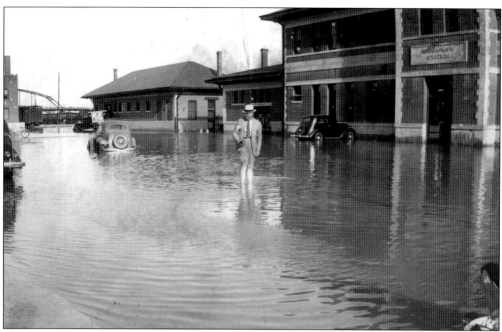

FLOODED TRAIN YARDS. The railroad tracks and depot parking lot are almost completely immersed in water during the torrential rains of 1939. (Bradshaw Collection, Heritage Museum.)

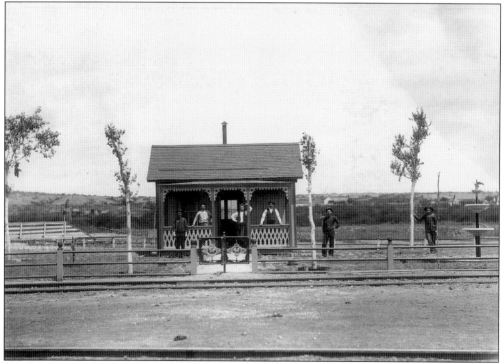

LITTLE HOUSE BY TRACKS. This little T&P house was built along the tracks next to the depot. (Heritage Museum.)

Six
It's a Gusher

The discovery of oil in 1925–26 pushed Big Spring, once again, into a booming town. Oil prices went from $1 to $3 a barrel, and gave a boost to Big Spring economy.

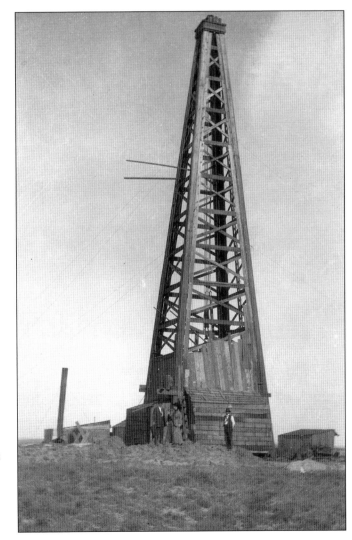

Wooden Oil Derrick, Quinn. This 1920 wooden oil derrick, Quinn Number 1, was located on the Quinn Ranch southwest of Big Spring. Pioneer builder Bascom Reagan built the derrick. (Cook Collection, Heritage Museum.)

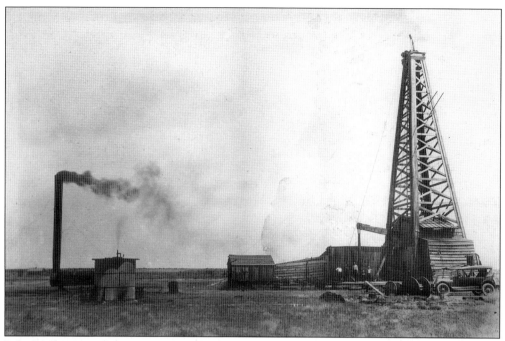

L.S. McDowell Ranch. One of the first oil wells in West Texas was drilled at the L.S. McDowell Ranch. S.E.J. Cox and the General Oil Co. drilled it in July 1920. (McDowell Collection, Heritage Museum.)

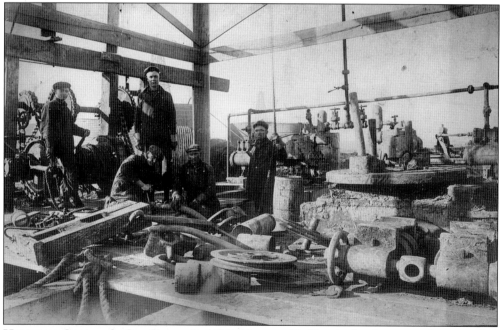

Houston Cowden's Oil Crew. In 1918, Houston D. Cowden's oil crew is shown with a rotary rig. (Cowden Collection, Heritage Museum.)

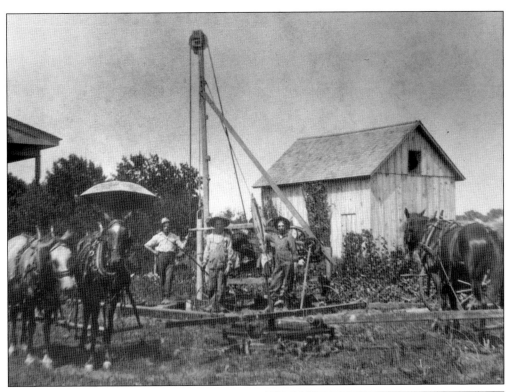

ROBINSON DRILLING CO. The Robinson Drilling Company used this horse-drawn oil well drilling rig in 1903. Through the years, Robinson's drilling rigs were vastly improved and became capable of drilling between 7,500 and 13,000-foot depths. (Robinson Collection, Heritage Museum.)

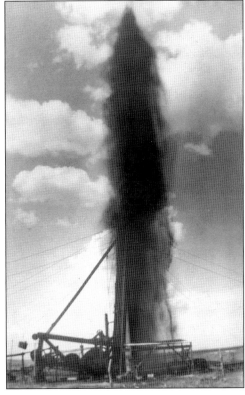

ROBINSON DRILLING. This cable tool rig was in use in the 1940s. The rig was used in the oilfield drilling operations of Robinson Drilling. (Robinson Collection, Heritage Museum.)

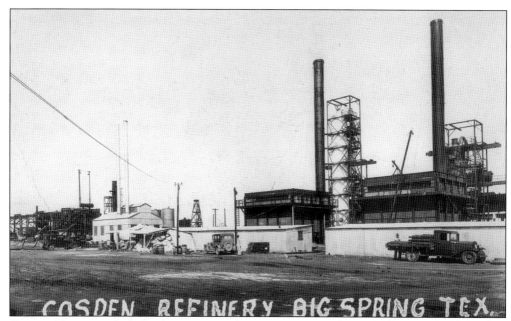

COSDEN REFINERY. Josh Cosden announced contracts on July 13, 1928, to build a 10,000-barrel refinery in Howard County. However, the stock market crashed in 1930 and Mr. Cosden developed a fatal lung disease. The company remained strong, but the cash to pay current debts was lacking. After a reorganization plan was approved in federal court, the transfer of properties was made to the Cosden Petroleum Corporation in 1937. (Heritage Museum.)

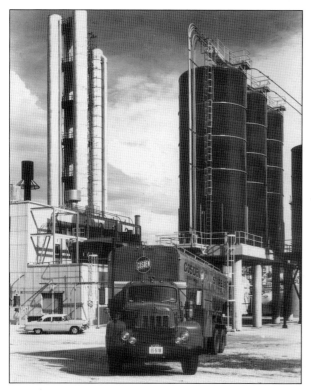

COSDEN TRANSPORT. In 1959, Cosden Oil and Chemical Company used one of the first custom designed transports for polystyrene in its local operation. Polystyrene silos, which contained polystyrene pellets, are show on the right. The plastics industry was revolutionized by use of polystyrene. (Cosden Collection, Heritage Museum.)

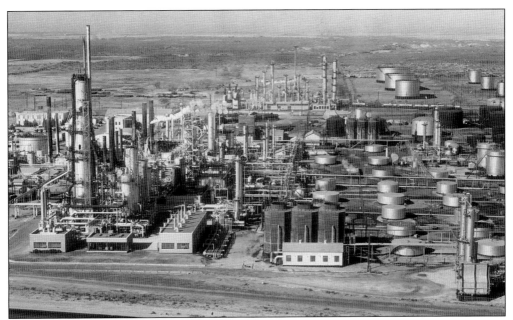

COSDEN REFINERY. This is a bird's eye view of Cosden Refinery taken by Bradshaw Studios in the 1950s. Raymond Tollett went to work at Cosden on July 16, 1939. He quickly became president and transformed the refinery into a vast industrial complex. Cosden was sold to Fina Oil and Chemical and is presently owned by Alon U.S.A. (Cosden Collection, Heritage Museum.)

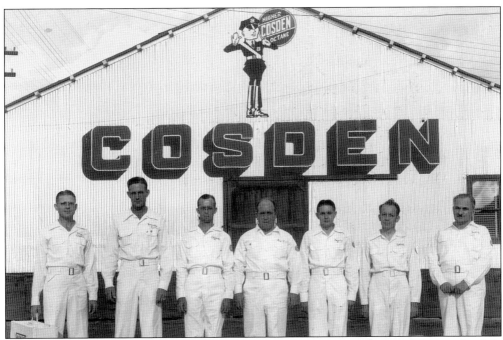

COSDEN FIRST AID TEAM. The Cosden First Aid Team included, from left to right, Mr. Morgan, Neal Barnaby, L.S. Edmonds Jr., unidentified, Lee Harris, J.A. Selkick, and Otto Peters Sr. (Cosden Collection, Heritage Museum.)

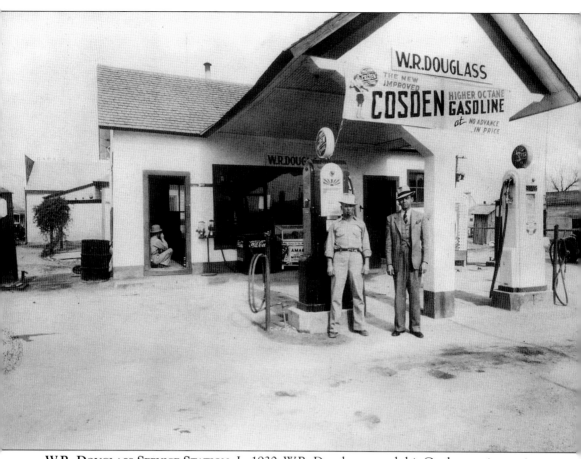

W.R. Douglass Service Station. In 1930, W.R. Douglass owned this Cosden service station at NW Second and Gregg Streets. (Heritage Museum.)

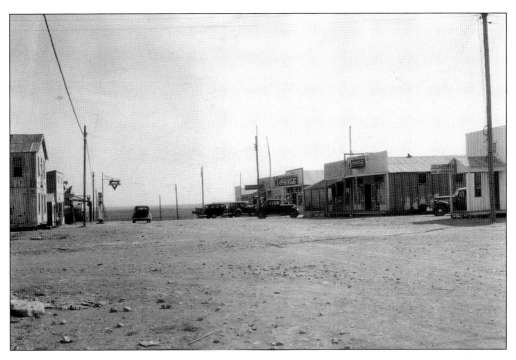

FORSAN TOWNSITE. On May 25, 1928, the town site of Forsan was placed on the market. The town site was located on the Clayton Stewart Ranch. An office was set up and lots were sold for $25 each, on a "first come, first serve" basis. In December 1928, the rapidly growing town was officially named Forsan. The name was derived from the fact that four paying oil sands were believed to be present in the area. In 1936, during Forsan's surge of oil growth, there were eight cafes in town. (Heritage Museum.)

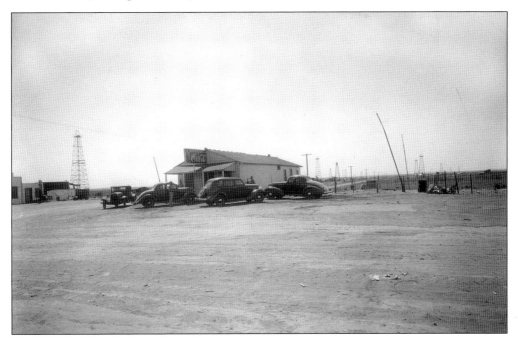

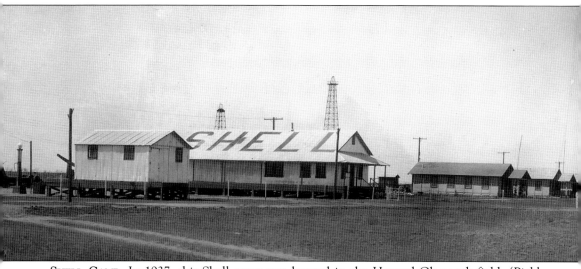

SHELL CAMP. In 1937, this Shell camp was located in the Howard Glasscock field. (Pickle Collection, Heritage Museum.)

Seven
WE PRAISE, LEARN, AND TEACH

Local residents took pride in their house of worship and their schools. They continued to improve them throughout the years for the betterment of souls and minds.

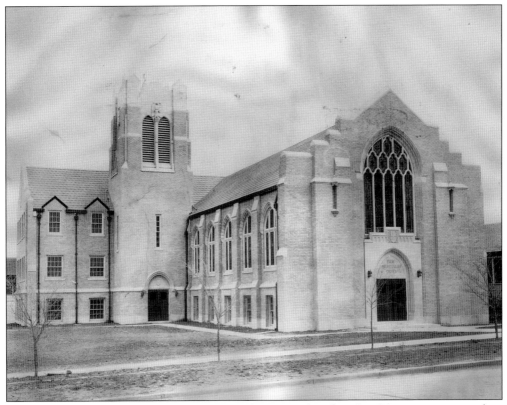

FIRST PRESBYTERIAN CHURCH. The First Presbyterian Church in Big Spring was organized on November 14, 1891. This beautiful new church was built on the corner of Seventh and Runnels Streets in 1929 for a cost of $70,000. New additions were added through the years. (Bradshaw Collection, Heritage Museum.)

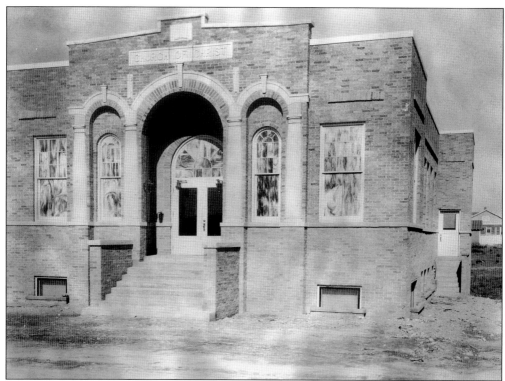

CHURCH OF CHRIST. In March 1929, services were conducted in the Church of Christ, at Fourteenth and Main Streets. The church's growth forced the congregation to make new additions including an auditorium, education building, and fellowship hall. (Bradshaw Collection, Heritage Museum.)

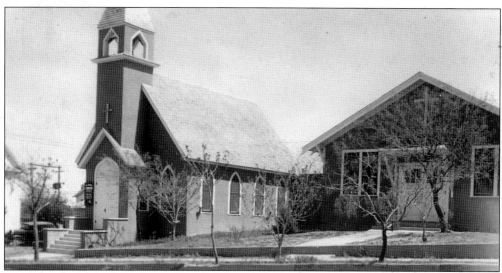

EPISCOPALIAN CHURCH. The Episcopalian church and Parish house were located at 501 Runnels Street. It was built in 1900, after a cyclone destroyed the original church building. The congregation moved into their new church home at 1001 Goliad in 1958. (Bradshaw Collection, Heritage Museum.)

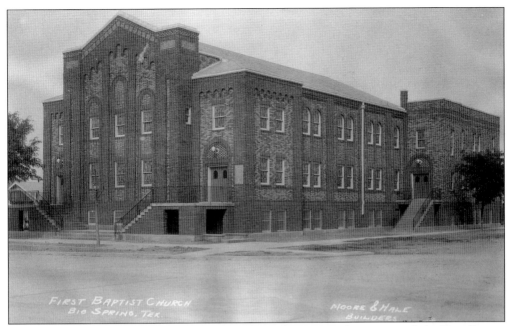

FIRST BAPTIST CHURCH. On October 24, 1928, a devastating fire consumed the First Baptist Church at Sixth and Main Street. Services were conducted in this new building for the first time on November 3, 1929. The old church building was torn down and the new post office was built. (Bradshaw Collection, Heritage Museum.)

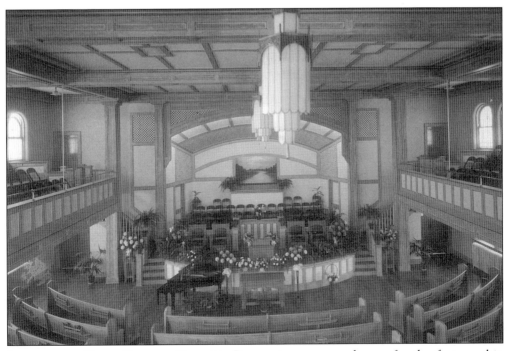

INTERIOR OF FIRST BAPTIST CHURCH. Preparations were underway for the first worship services in the newly completed First Baptist Church. (Bradshaw Collection, Heritage Museum.)

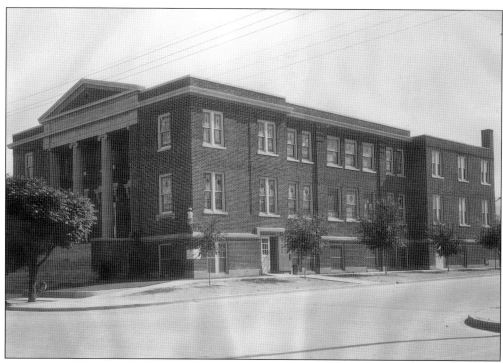

METHODIST CHURCH. The Methodist Church was the first church in Howard County to be organized. The first building was erected in 1884 at Fourth and Scurry Streets. The building was torn down in 1923 and replaced with this new modern structure, with several additions built on throughout the years. (Bradshaw Collection, Heritage Museum.)

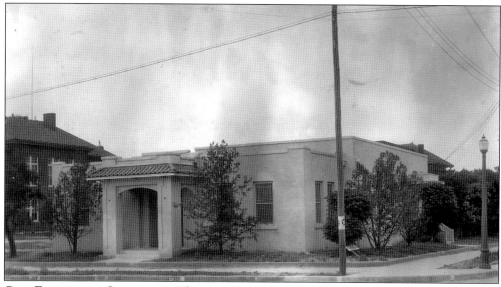

CITY FEDERATION CLUBHOUSE. The new City Federation Clubhouse was completed in 1929 at 311 Scurry. It was located on the corner of the courthouse grounds. The library moved in and shared the building. (Bradshaw Collection, Heritage Museum.)

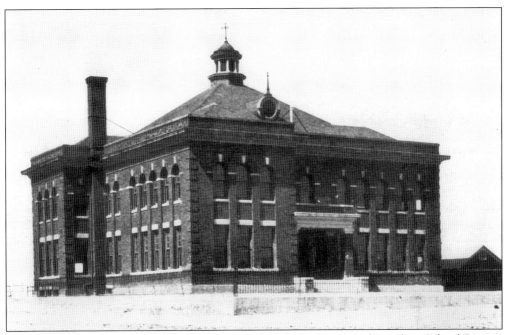

CENTRAL WARD. The first building constructed by the Big Spring Independent School District was Central Ward. It was a lovely red brick building erected in 1902 between Third and Fourth Streets on Scurry. The new building housed 10 grades, and consisted of 8 classrooms and a superintendent's office. The building was enclosed with an iron fence. In 1916, the high school students moved into the newly built Big Spring High School (Runnels). Elementary students continued to attend school at the Ward location until 1931, at which time Central Ward was razed to make room for the new post office. (Heritage Museum.)

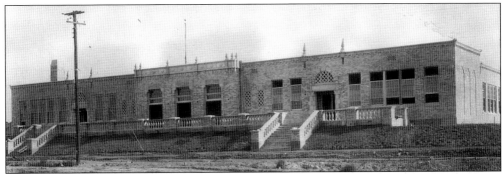

WEST WARD ELEMENTARY. West Ward Elementary School was built in 1930 at West Eighth Street between Douglas and Aylesford Streets. The center classroom in the front of the building was larger than the other classrooms. A beautiful fireplace decorated with ceramic tiles was centered in the room. In 1966, the name of the school was changed to Cedar Crest because of the numerous mountain cedar trees in the area. The school closed in 1977 and torn down in 1982. (Bradshaw Collection, Heritage Museum.)

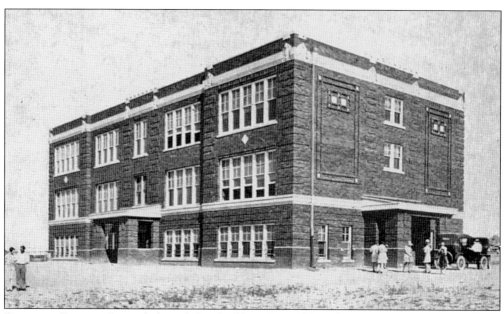

RUNNELS SCHOOL. It was believed that building Central Ward in 1902 would eliminate over crowded schools. Big Spring was experiencing a population boom and soon became desperate again for more classroom space. A new high school was erected at the end of Runnels and Tenth Streets. The first phase of the building was completed in 1916 and the second addition was added to the side of the original building in 1928. The gym was added on to the east side of the campus in 1938. This photo shows the first phase shortly after its completion. (Alderman Collection, Heritage Museum.)

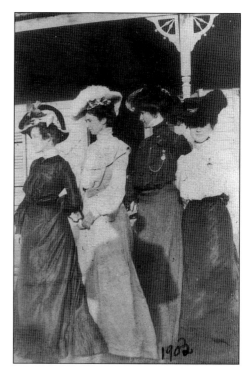

SCHOOL MAR'MS. These 1903 school mar'ms are dressed in their finest attire. They often set the pace, not only in education, but also in style for early day Big Spring women. The school mar'm was expected to have a neat appearance, set a high standard of personal decorum, participate in community affairs, and work for meager salaries. Pictured here are, from left to right, Miss Addie Hyde, Miss Carrie Russell, Miss Della K. Russell, and Miss Fay Gorman. (Agnell Collection, Heritage Museum.)

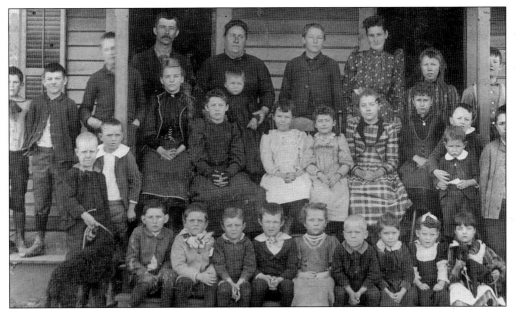

INKMAN SCHOOL. Mrs. W.J. Inkman grew up in a Catholic convent in St. Louis and was a talented musician. Education was extremely important to her and she was fluent in French, Spanish, German, and Latin. She taught all of the children to play the piano and at least one string instrument. Mrs. Inkman taught the local children school in her home at 204 Johnston Street. In this picture, taken c. 1889–90, Mr. and Mrs. Inkman are on the top row among her students and Ralph Dietz's dog. (Pickle Collection, Heritage Museum.)

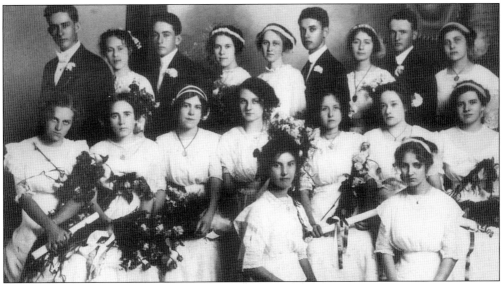

CENTRAL WARD GRADUATING CLASS. Pictured here is Central Ward High School's graduating class of 1912. In the front row are Ninetta Parker and Alta Vaughan; the middle row, Margaret Patty, Ellen Ingham, Eloise Roberts, Mabel Hatch, Gladys Orenbaum, Verna Mauldin, and Leona Fisher; and in the back are Brown Alexander, Bernice Devenport, George Whittington, Ona Reagan, Jessie Wilson, Karl Harris, Velma Wasson, Norman Reed, and Florence Willis. (Heritage Museum.)

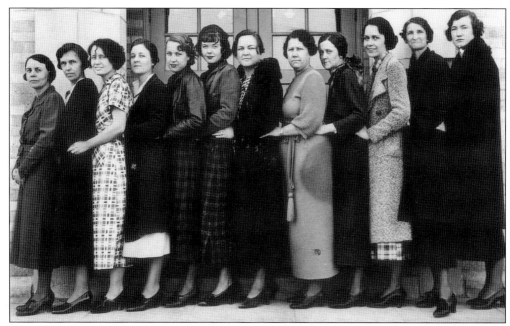

WEST WARD FACULTY. The West Ward faculty line up for photographs, c. 1934–35. The teachers are, from left to right, Theo Sullivan, Jane Odom, Cloe Stripling, Emma Baker, Delores Crain, Abadell Mannerly, Zoe Hardy Parks, Ruth Miller Rutherford, Sallie Jordon Wasson, Georgie Fowler, Della K. Agnell, and Naomi Lee Stephens. (Agnell Collection, Heritage Museum.)

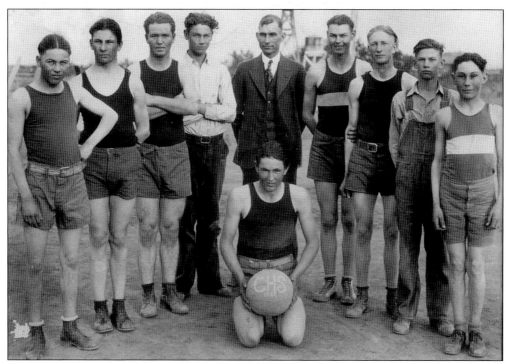

COAHOMA BASKETBALL TEAM. This is the Coahoma boy's basketball team in 1927. (Breyman Collection, Heritage Museum.)

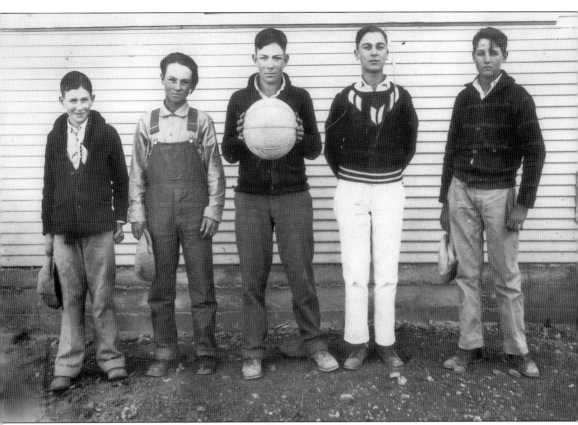

CHALK BASKETBALL TEAM. The 1927–28 Chalk basketball team consisted of five players, left to right: Johnny Prude, Alfred Coplin, Carey Prude, Knox Smith, and Fred Warner. (Early Collection, Heritage Museum.)

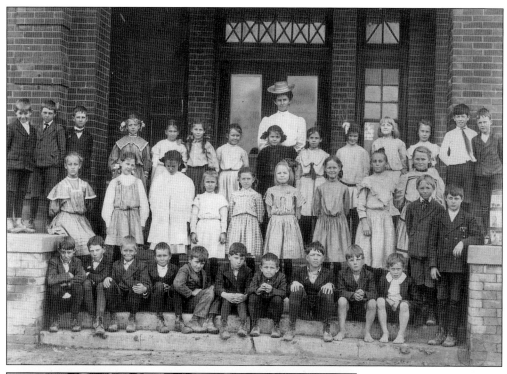

CENTRAL WARD SECOND GRADE. Miss Annie Pope (teacher) proudly stands behind her second grade class at Central Ward School on March 17, 1908. (Middleton Collection, Heritage Museum.)

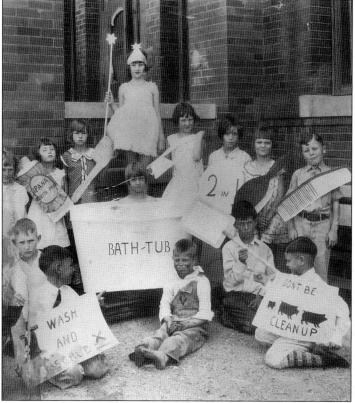

"KEEP CLEAN." Students presented the "Keep Clean" program from Central Ward School. (Agnell Collection, Heritage Museum.)

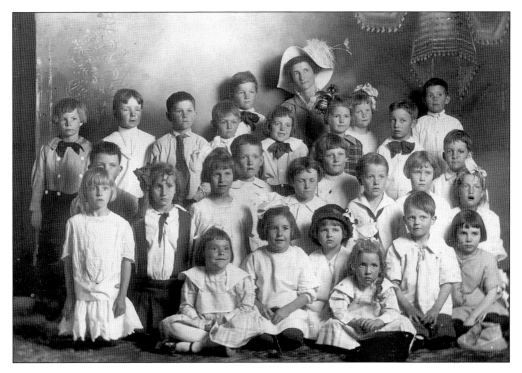

Two Photos of Agnell School. Mrs. Della Agnell began a "private school" in her home at 311 W. Sixth Street (previously 601 Jack). She began with "overflow" first grade students from the public school, who were referred to her by the superintendent, Mr. Brasher. It was called the Big Spring Primary School. Tuition was $3 per month, unless a child missed due to whooping cough or measles. In that case, there was no charge for that month. (Agnell Collection, Heritage Museum.)

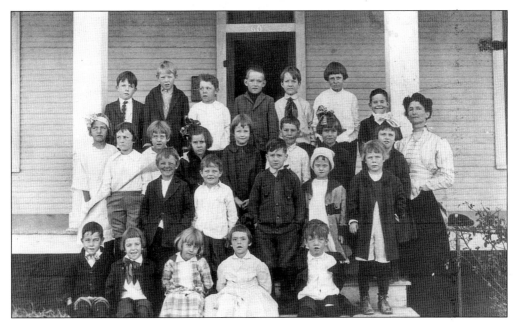

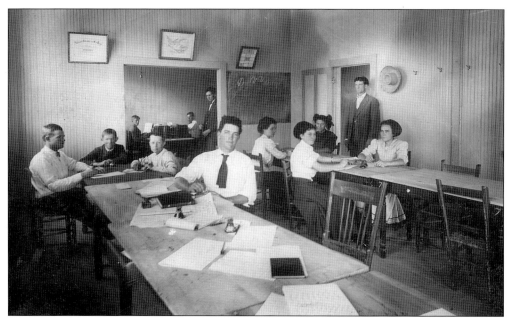

BUSINESS COLLEGE. In 1912, the Business College was located upstairs in this Main Street building. The building later became the Albert M. Fisher Store. (Wasson Collection, Heritage Museum.)

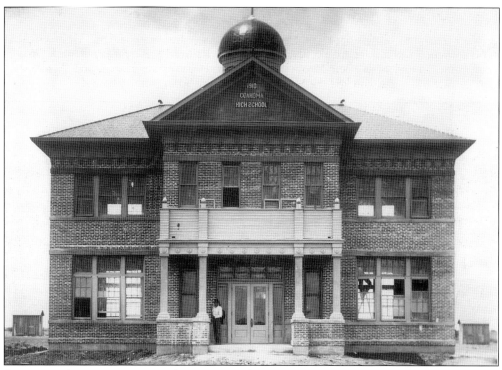

COAHOMA SCHOOL. In 1909, this two-story brick structure was being built to replace the Coahoma school building, which was destroyed by fire. (Rhoton Collection, Heritage Museum.)

Eight
HOTEL, MOTEL, AND TOURIST COURTS

Many "famous folks" stopped off in Big Spring for a little rest and relaxation, such as Lawrence Welk, Ellen Gould (daughter of T&P Railroad president Jay Gould), Gregory Peck, former president Herbert Hoover and his son, PGA Walter Hagen, and "Wrongway" Carrigan are just a few who laid their heads to rest in Big Spring's finest hotels.

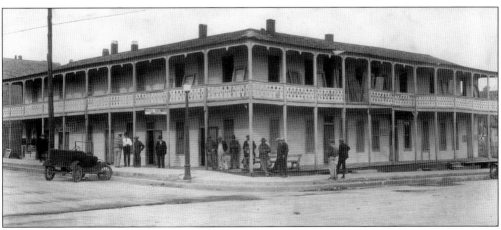

STEWART HOTEL. Workers prepare for the Hotel Stewart's demise in 1928. The hotel was once home to the Earl of Aylesford, who according to local legend, bought the hotel when they did not have a room available for him to rent. It was then known as the Cosmopolitan Hotel. It was located at the corner of Third and Runnels streets. (Bradshaw Collection, Heritage Museum.)

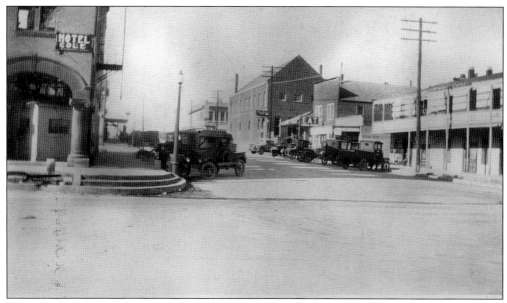

TEARING DOWN THE STEWART. In 1927, the Stewart Hotel was in the process of being razed (right) and the Cole Hotel had just burned down (left), leaving Big Spring desperately in need of temporary lodging for the weary traveler. (Bradshaw Collection, Heritage Museum.)

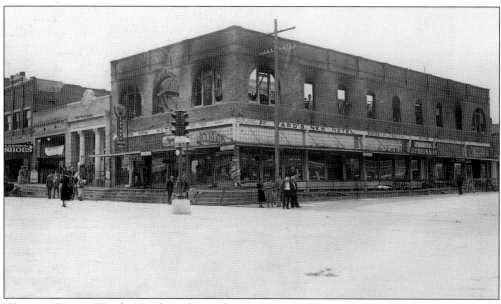

WARD'S HOTEL. Ward's Hotel was located at the corner of Second and Main streets. After the hotel burned in the 1930s, a new building was erected and became home to McCrory's Variety Store. (Heritage Museum.)

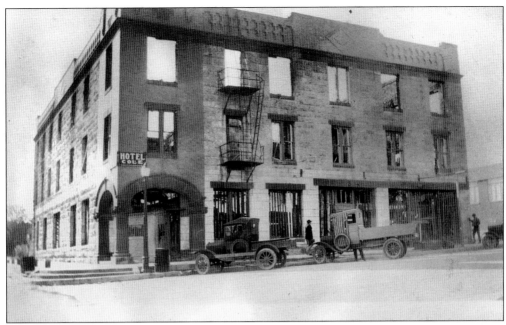

COLE HOTEL. The Cole Hotel, built by W.R. Cole in 1909, stood at the corner of Runnels and East Third Street. The contractor was J.M. Morgan, a local mason, who used limestone salvaged from the former courthouse. The hotel had three floors and was one of the finest in Big Spring. The $1 rate was extremely high in the 1920s but despite the fee, several Big Spring residents would go there just to take a "running water" bath on special occasions. The hotel fell victim to a devastating fire on December 17, 1926, that consumed the building. (Heritage Museum.)

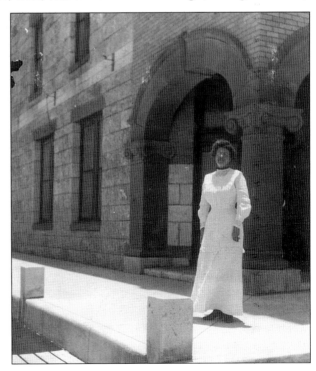

ANNA PANCOAST IN FRONT OF COLE HOTEL. Anna Pancoast stands in front of the Cole Hotel in 1910. She and her husband George L. Pancoast managed the hotel for W.R. Cole. (Pancoast Collection, Heritage Museum.)

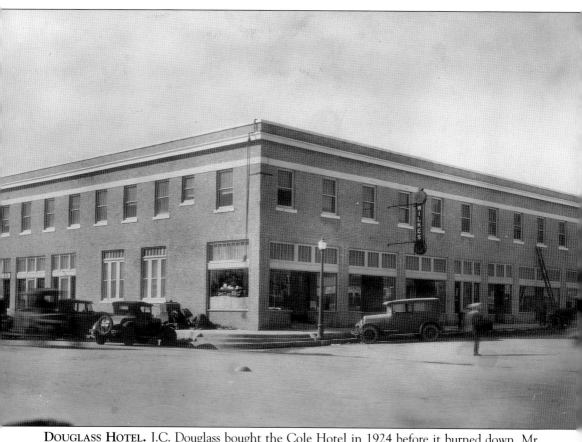

Douglass Hotel. J.C. Douglass bought the Cole Hotel in 1924 before it burned down. Mr. Douglass had insurance on the building and was able to entice investors to rebuild the hotel with the stipulation that the hotel be bigger than before. The first unit was completed for the March 16, 1928, formal opening. (Heritage Museum.)

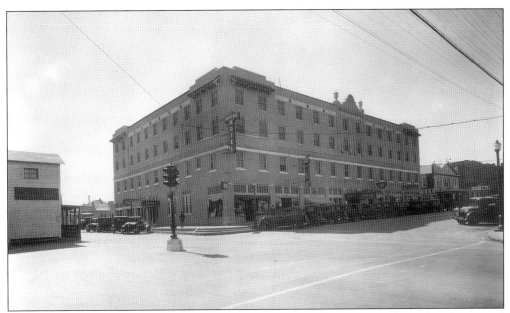

DOUGLASS HOTEL AT COMPLETION. The Douglass Hotel became complete after the second unit was added in 1929. The exterior of the building was cream brick and white trim. Terrazzo floors were used in the corridors and the hotel lobby, and over half the rooms had adjoining bathrooms. The hotel was the pride and joy of the J.C. Douglass family, as well as Big Spring residents. (Bradshaw Collection, Heritage Museum.)

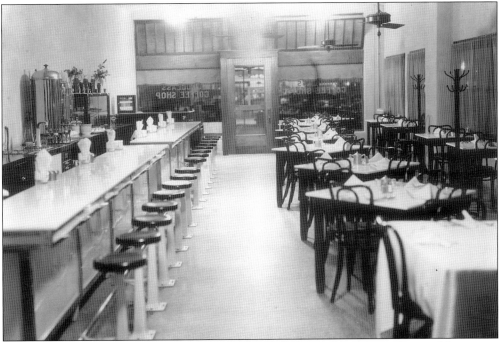

DOUGLASS COFFEE SHOP. The ground floor of the Douglass Hotel housed several businesses including a barbershop, beauty parlor, ladies dress shop, jewelry and optical shop, and the Douglass Coffee Shop. (Bradshaw Collection, Heritage Museum.)

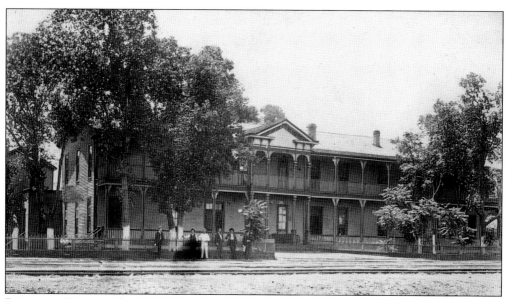

BIRDWELL HOTEL. The T&P Hotel, built shortly before 1889, was also called the Birdwell Hotel, and was operated by John D. Birdwell. The Y.M.C.A. was directly west of the hotel; both were located on First Street, facing the railroad tracks. The lobby served as the ticket office and waiting room for the railroad. This photo was taken in 1896. Mrs. L.S. McDowell remembered when she first arrived in Big Spring. "We stepped off the train into the Birdwell Hotel, and all night long I thought it rained, but in the morning found it was only the wind whispering softly among the leaves of the cottonwood trees that surrounded and hovered over the hotel." (Heritage Museum.)

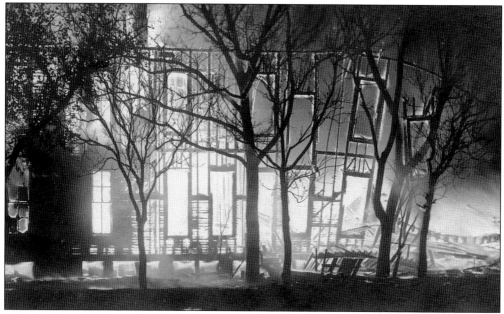

BIRDWELL HOTEL ON FIRE. In the fall of 1908, flames engulfed the T&P (Birdwell) Hotel, completely destroying the building. A train depot for the T&P Railroad was erected on the former sight of the hotel. (Heritage Museum.)

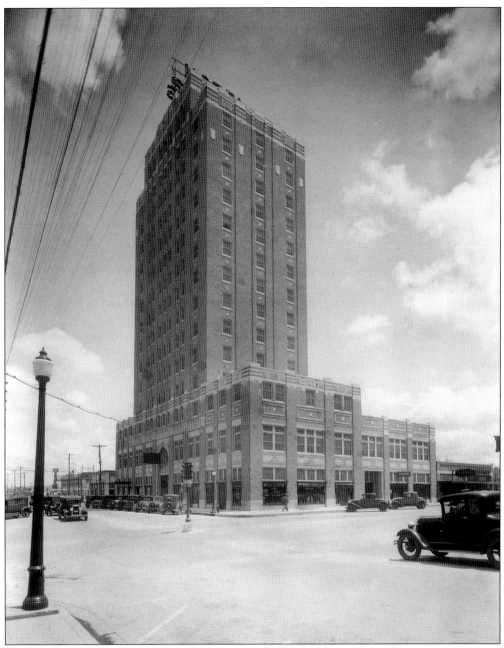

SETTLES HOTEL. Mr. and Mrs. W.R. Settles built the Settles Hotel in 1930 at the cost of $500,000. The hotel was built of the grandest scale. Room rates were $2 to $3 with an advertised capacity for 300 guests. Each of the 170 guest rooms had a bath and shower. During the Great Depression, oil dropped from $4 a barrel to 10¢. Mr. and Mrs. Settles lost their entire 10-section ranch they had put up to secure the hotel. With a debt of over $118,000.00, the Settles Hotel was foreclosed. Slowly the parties and dances disappeared, and the hotel continued to change owners regularly. Eventually it was stripped, piece by piece and sold off to the highest bidder, leaving an empty shell of what was once the most elegant hotel in the West. (Bradshaw collection, Heritage Museum.)

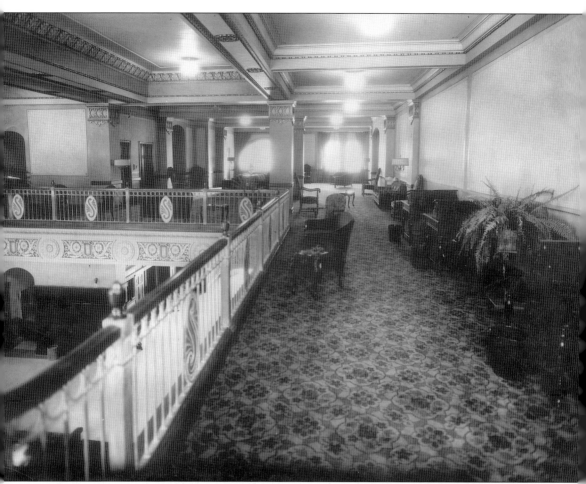

SECOND FLOOR OF THE SETTLES HOTEL. A grand staircase from the lobby to the second floor mezzanine (shown) was finished with green marble risers. A painted wrought iron rail ran from the foot of the stairs and continued around the promenade. The scrolled letter "S" was placed in the middle of each wrought iron section. (Bradshaw Collection, Heritage Museum.)

CRAWFORD HOTEL. (*opposite page, top photo*) Across from the Courthouse on Third Street, construction began on the Crawford Hotel on April 29, 1927, and a grand opening was slated for Thanksgiving Day of the same year. The reputable Calvin Boykin served the Crawford as manger. The hotel was elegantly decorated, from the fumed oak on the walls to the brass doorknobs monogrammed with interlinked C&H initials. The Crawford had the only electric elevator in Big Spring in 1927. At one time there had to be guards posted outside of the hotel to keep the school children from playing on them. The great hotel was abandoned and closed in 1963, and on October 23, 1968, it was destroyed for a parking lot. (Bradshaw collection, Heritage Museum.)

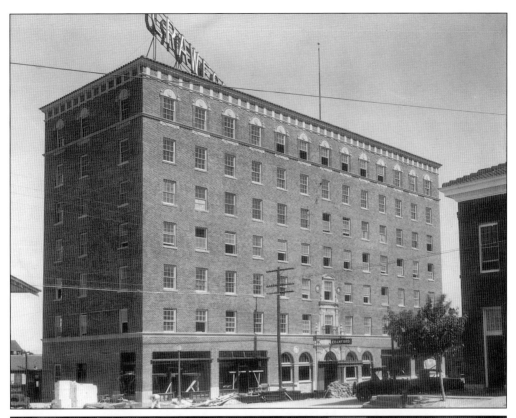

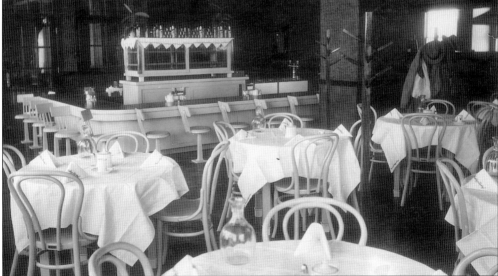

INTERIOR OF CRAWFORD COFFEE SHOP. Crescent Drug Company, Big Spring Chamber of Commerce, a beauty shop, The Yellow Cab Company, and the Crawford Coffee Shop were all located on the ground floor of the Crawford Hotel. The coffee shop was always impeccable. Each table was dressed with a linen tablecloth, linen napkins, monogrammed with the Crawford name, a crystal water carafe, and dishes with the Crawford seal. (Bradshaw Collection, Heritage Museum.)

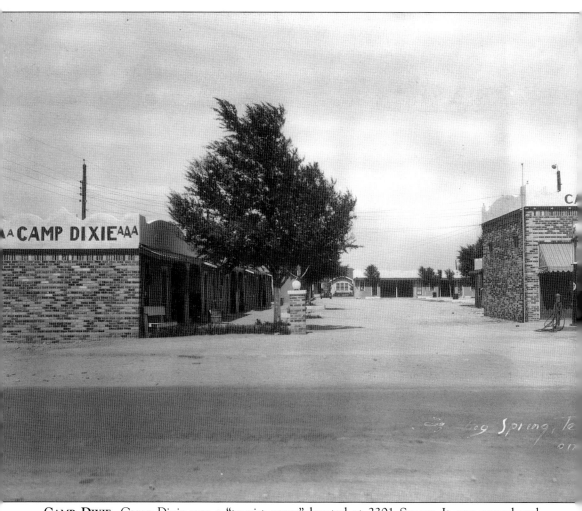

CAMP DIXIE. Camp Dixie was a "tourist camp" located at 2301 Scurry. It was owned and operated by O.H. McAlister. The camp consisted of a "Kash and Karry" store and a Conoco gas

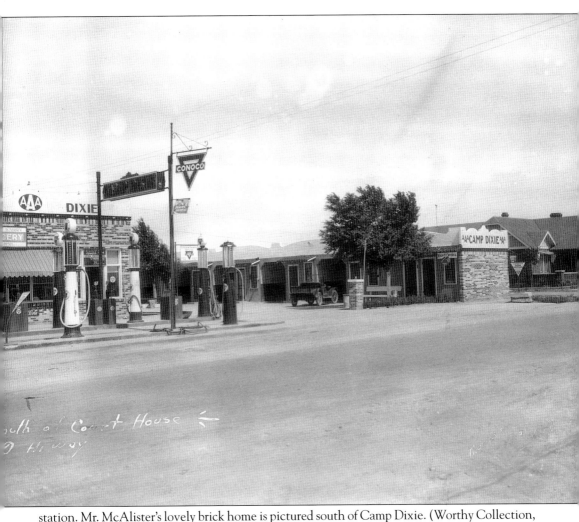

station. Mr. McAlister's lovely brick home is pictured south of Camp Dixie. (Worthy Collection, Heritage Museum.)

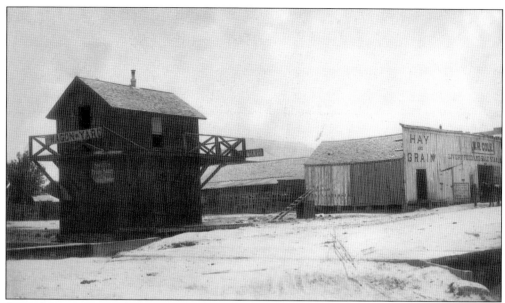

COLE CAMP HOUSE. The overnight camp house at the Cole Wagon Yard was where friends met with friends after long days spent on the roads in wagons. The women slept upstairs and the men slept in the downstairs area. The Camp House was located at the corner of East Third and Runnels streets. It was owned by W.R. Cole, who later built and operated the Cole Hotel. (Cole Collection, Heritage Museum.)

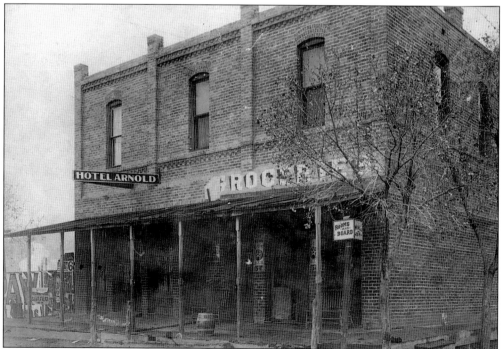

HOTEL ARNOLD. The Hotel Arnold was located at 102 South First Street in Coahoma. A small grocery store was in the building and it later became the Padgett Hotel and Phillip Grocery. (Heritage Museum.)

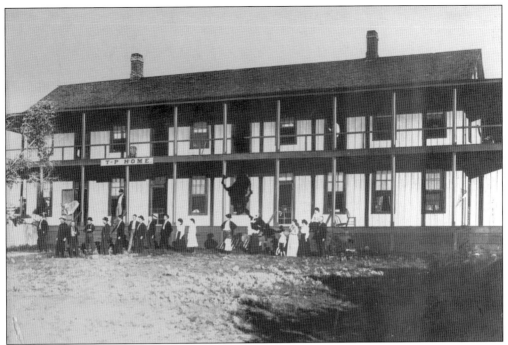

T&P Railroad Hotel. Ed Tucker built the T&P Home at 301 West First Street (West of Gregg Street.) Can Powell operated the home for the T&P Railroad to house its employees until they could build homes. Mr. Powell did not wait for the guests to come to the hotel; he would go to the trains and introduce himself as they got off. In 1909, John Millhollon and his wife Sarah became the new proprietors of the hotel. (Heritage Museum.)

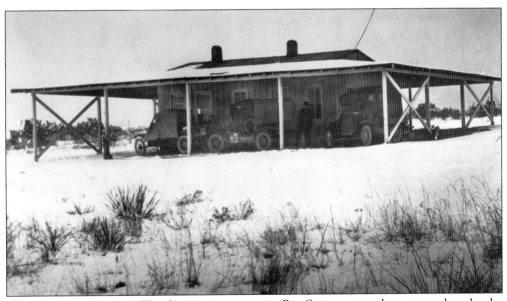

First Tourist Camp. The first tourist camp in Big Spring catered to a new breed—the automobile tourist. It was located at 1500 Scurry, which was the old San Angelo Highway. This tourist camp was a project with the Business Men's Club, which would provide free lodging to visitors. The Club later became the Big Spring Chamber of Commerce. (Heritage Museum.)

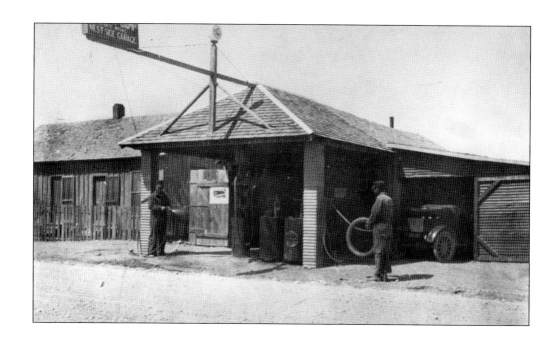

TOURIST CAMP IN JONES VALLEY. This tourist camp was located on West Third Street in Jones Valley. It was remodeled to accommodate the automobile traveler. Mr. C.M. Grissham operated the Tourist Camp and West Side Garage. (Grissham Collection, Heritage Museum.)

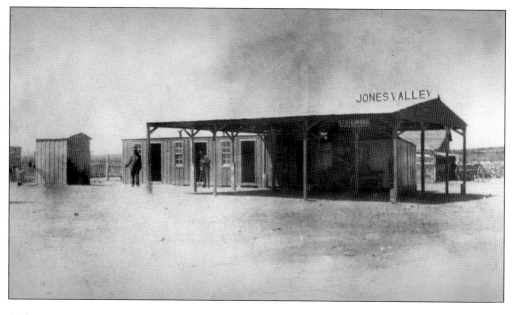

Nine
LET THE GOOD TIMES ROLL

Hard work had to be rewarded with a little playtime. From patriotic parades to picnics with sweethearts, everyone was ready for a relaxing and enjoyable time.

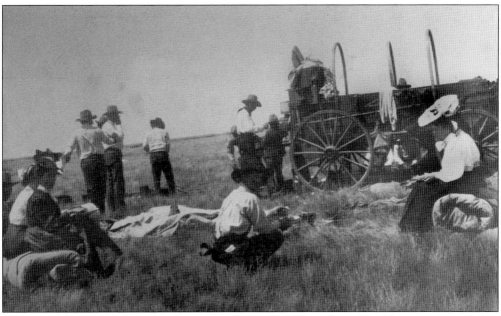

DINNER ON THE GROUND. Sundays were often called "Sweetheart Day" because young ladies from town would dress in their finery and ride out to visit the cowboys on the ranch. In 1906, at German Springs–Slaughter Ranch, the ladies sat on bed rolls while the men enjoyed home cooking. (Heritage Museum.)

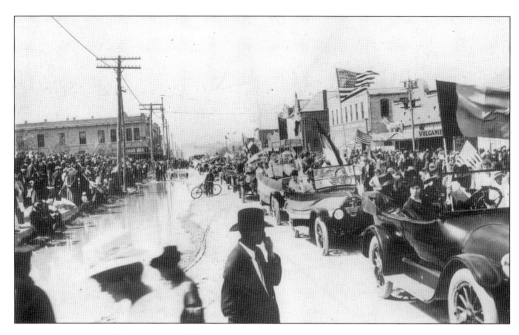

PARADES IN BIG SPRING. In 1917, patriotic fever was at a high pitch. America had been plunged into a war, which President Wilson said was waged to make the world safe for democracy. (Heritage Museum.)

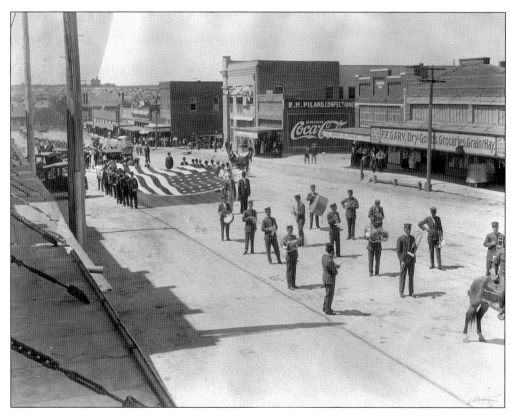

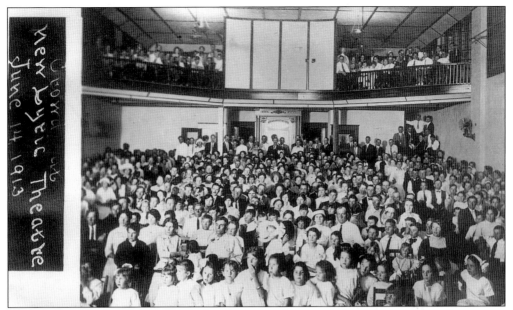

LYRIC THEATRE. On June 14, 1913, Big Spring residents turned out in their finest for opening night at the Lyric theatre. The theatre's seating capacity of 400 was completely full. Local moviegoers spent Saturday mornings with "Hoot Gibson or Tom Mix," and paid 25¢ for that pleasure.

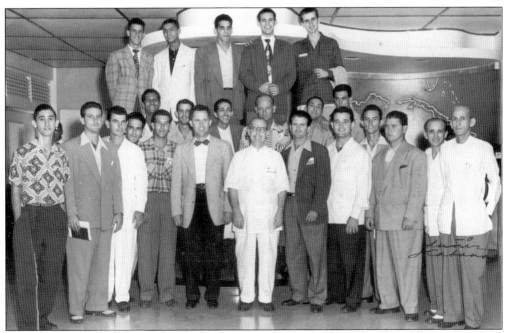

CUBAN BASEBALL PLAYERS. The Washington Senators Baseball Team sent scouts to Cuba in order to recruit young, talented baseball players. In 1951, Aramis (Tito) Arencibia, pictured third in middle row, and brothers Danny and Al Valdez, on bottom row left to right, were sent to Big Spring to play in a branch team named the Broncs. After some financial difficulties, the Broncs sponsorship was taken over by R.L. Tollett and Cosden. (Courtesy of Tito Arencibia)

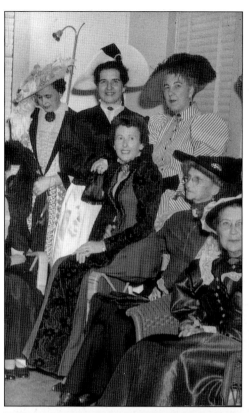

HYPERION CLUB. The 1905 Hyperion Club of Big Spring was organized in January 1905. The purpose of the club was to promote and stimulate intellectual growth among its members. The club worked to install playgrounds and sanitary drinking fountains in the schools, to abolish the public drinking cup, and successfully organized the first public library. In 1955, the club celebrated 50 years. Pictured left to right are: Mrs. Tony Hunt, Mrs. Tracey Smith, Mrs. Shine Philips, Mrs. Charles Long, Mrs. Della Agnell, and Mrs. Norman Read. (1905 Hyperion, Heritage Museum.)

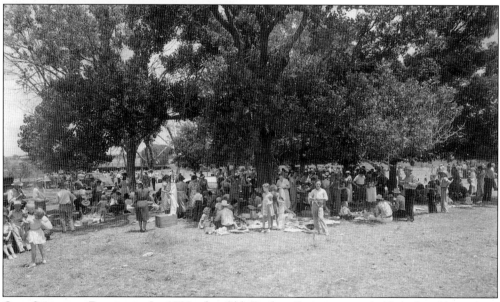

OLD SETTLERS REUNION. In 1939, the Old Settlers Reunion was held under the trees at Cottonwood Park, also known as Roopers Grove or Parrish Park. Later the Old Settlers moved their reunion to the covered pavilion at Comanche Trail Park. The gathering of settlers began in 1924 and was soon known as the Howard-Glasscock County Old Settler's Reunion. (Heritage Museum.)

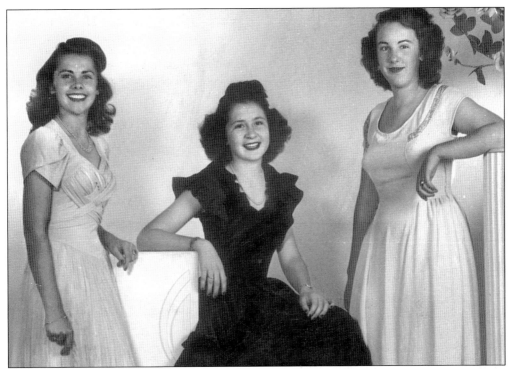

1945 SUBS. Twelve pledges were presented to society in 1945. Three of those pledges were left to right: Cecilia Long, Betty Lou McGinnis, and Patricia Curry. A spotlight shone on each Sub as she was announced by stepping from a decorated heart onto the stage. Over 600 people attended this very formal affair at the Municipal Auditorium. (Bradshaw Collection, Heritage Museum.)

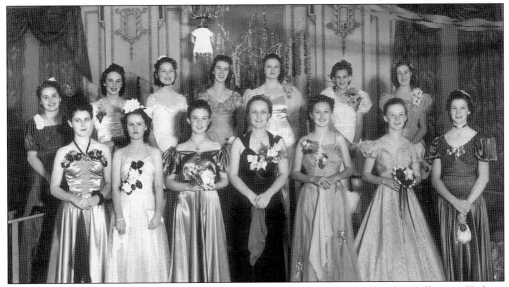

1938 SUBS. In November 1938, Subs were presented at the elegant Settles Ballroom. To be a "Sub" was a high honor bestowed to a limited number of pledges. (Bradshaw Collection, Heritage Museum.)

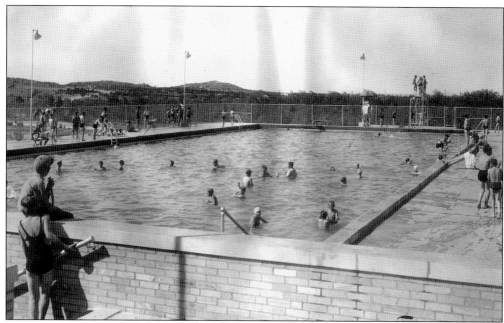

THE MUNICIPAL NATATORIUM. The swimming pool, or natatorium as the citizens had learned to call it, was completed by the PWA, November 1, 1935. It required "nine hours to pump the 405,000 gallons of water into the pool." The "Municipal Natatorium" was opened to the public on April 24, 1936. (Bradshaw Collection, Heritage Museum.)

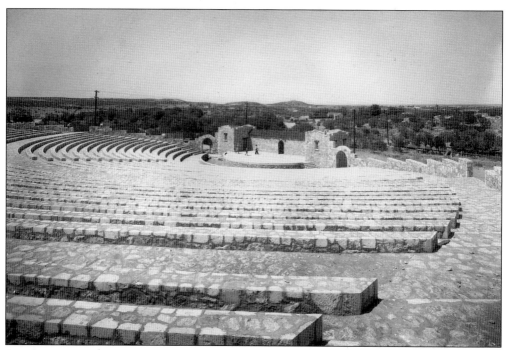

BIG SPRING AMPHITHEATER. The WPA built this classical structure to seat 3,000. However, they later decided to increase the seating capacity to 6,000 in order to better serve a town of this size. The Big Spring City Park Amphitheater was completed in 1938. (Heritage Museum.)

Ten
WORLD WAR I TO WEBB A.F.B.

Big Spring residents have always eagerly supported their country. During World War I, a parade marched the boys to the train for their send off to France. The Big Spring Bombardier School was opened during World War II. After the war, The Big Spring Army Air Field was activated on October 1, 1951, to train pilots. In 1952, Big Spring A.F.B. was officially re-named Webb Air Force Base in honor of 1st Lt. James L. Webb, a local F-51 fighter pilot who lost his life during a crash in Japan in 1949. When it was announced on March 30, 1977, that Webb would be closed, Big Spring residents and officials rallied together in a hard-fought battle to save it. The headlines cried, "Losing Webb Was Like Losing a Good Friend."

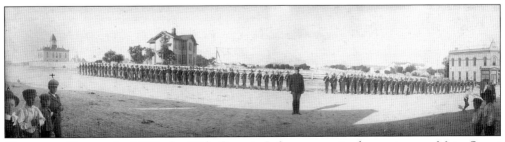

GEORGIAN TROOP. In 1899, the 29th Georgia Infantry practiced exercises on Main Street during the troop's train layover. The soldiers were on their way to the Philippine Islands. (Read Collection, Heritage Museum.)

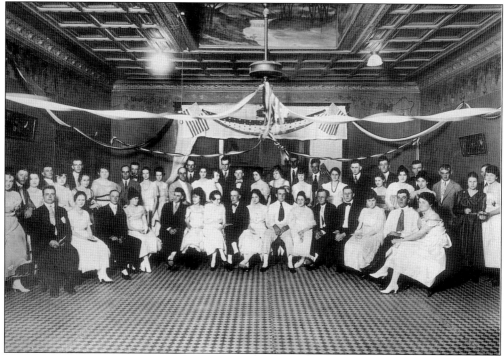

COLE HOTEL DANCE. On August 1, 1917, a spirited rendition of "Over There" was sung throughout the night at the Cole Hotel dining room. A dance was held in honor of the Motor Truck Company D, 117th Supply Train, before they were shipped off to France. (Robb Collection, Heritage Museum.)

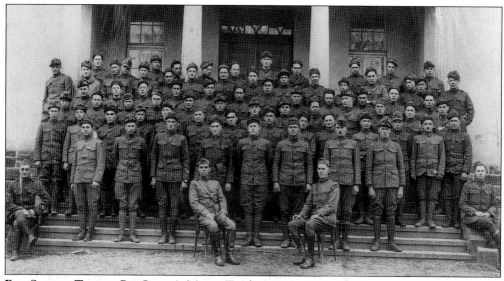

BIG SPRING TROOP. Big Spring's Motor Truck Company No. 4, Company D, 117th Supply Train, of the 4 Second Division, also known as the Rainbow Division, boarded the train on August 9, 1917, and made their way to France to serve their country. The Company Commander was 1st Lt. James T. Brooks. The Rainbow Division had its 19th Annual Reunion on August 9, 1936. (Bradshaw Collection, Heritage Museum.)

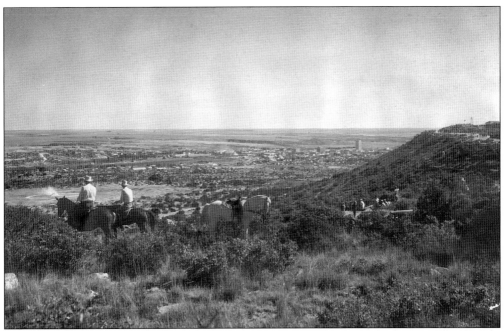

BOMB TARGET SIGHT. In 1943, Raymond Tollett and C.T. McLaughlin watch on horseback as students of the Big Spring Bombardier School practice dropping bombs on a target site where Scenic Mountain Medical Center is now located. From 1942 to 1946, the Bombardier School produced over 5,000 bombardiers; hundreds were decorated for exceptional valor. (Bradshaw Collection, Heritage Museum.)

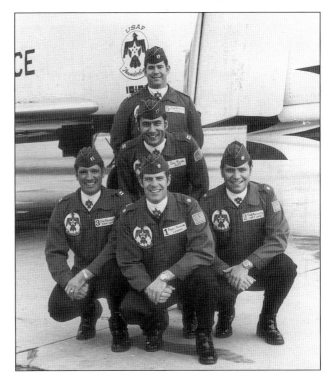

THUNDERBIRDS. On April 1, 1973, the elite thunderbird fighter pilots pose in formation. Pictured here are, left to right: (bottom row) right wing, Rip Blasdell; leader, Roger Parrish; left wing, Nels Rumming; slot, Tim Roells; and (top) Sold Kirk Brimmer. (U.S.A.F. Collection, Heritage Museum.)

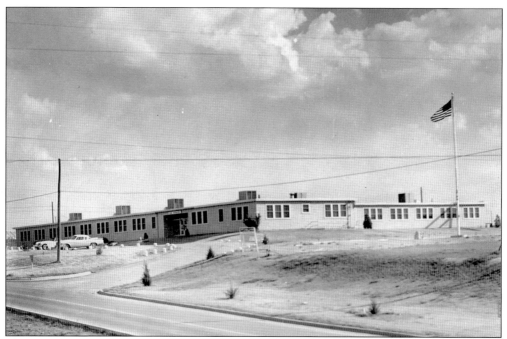

WING HEADQUARTERS. One of the first stops made at Webb Air Force Base was usually to the Wing Headquarters. It was the administrative offices of the Wing Commander and his staff. (U.S.A.F. Collection, Heritage Museum.)

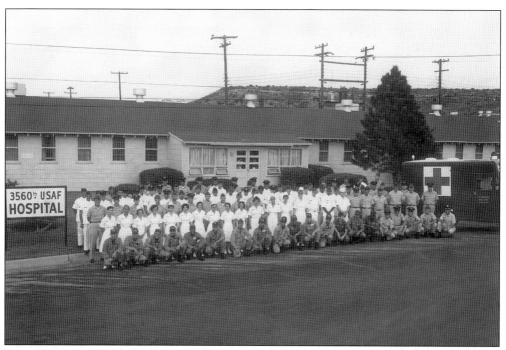

BASE HOSPITAL. Webb Air Force Base Hospital celebrates 25 years of service to their country. (U.S.A.F. Collection, Heritage Museum.)

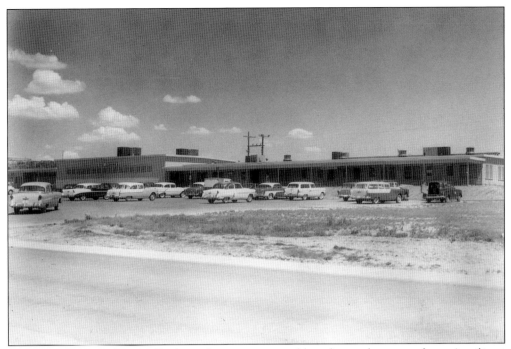

BASE EXCHANGE. The Base Exchange's main store was like other exchanges on base. A military I.D. card was required by each individual in order to enter the store. The store offered clothing, toiletries, and various essentials to a service man or his family, at slightly above cost. Additional concessions operated by the exchange included a tailor shop, laundry, cleaners, optical shop, beauty shop, and barbershop. (U.S.A.F. Collection, Heritage Museum.)

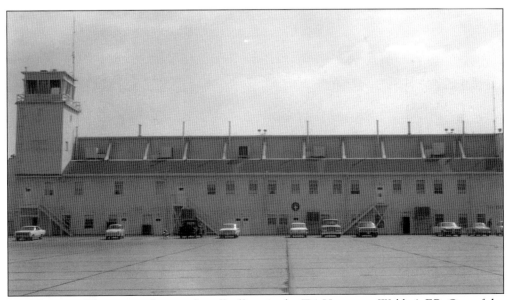

T-1 HANGER. There were dozens of small offices in the T-1 Hanger at Webb A.F.B. One of the busiest was the maintenance control office. This office was the nerve center for all maintenance work done at Webb. Any repairs to the aircraft on the flight lines or in the many shops in the field were handled through this office. (U.S.A.F. Collection, Heritage Museum.)

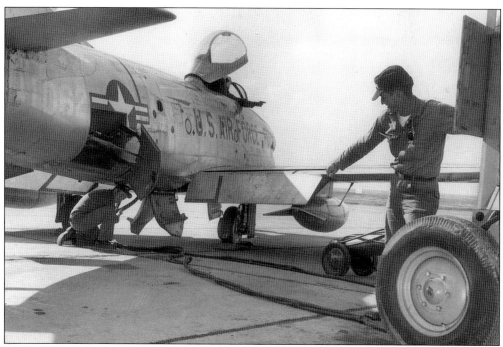

JETS BEING FUELED. A jet is being fueled on the tarmac at Webb A.F.B. (U.S.A.F. Collection, Heritage Museum.)

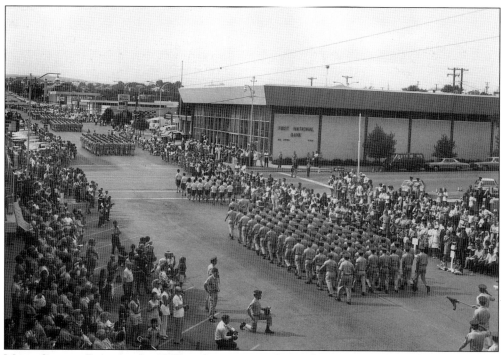

MAIN STREET PARADE. In 1967, military personal march up Main Street during the 25th anniversary of Webb A.F.B. By August 1977, the last two classes of students left Webb Air Force Base one final time. (W.A.F.B. Collection, Heritage Museum.)